FROM HALF TO WHOLE

A journey to overcome the battle scars of
adoption and living to tell about it

ಶಂಡಾ

REGINA RADOMSKI

WITH

BARBARA JEAN KEANE, M.S.W., L.C.S.W.

FROM HALF TO WHOLE

ISBN-13: 978-1480076310
ISBN-10: 1480076317

LCCN 2013917725

The names and locations in this book have been changed to protect the identities of the parties involved.

This book was produced using PressBooks.com; PDF rendering by PrinceXML. Printed in the United States of America

1 3 5 7 9 10 8 6 4 2

I am honored that you asked me to read your book before its final publishing.
As I read each page, so many emotions came over me—
happiness, sadness, fear, sorrow, joy, frustration and delight. . . .
I cried, I laughed, I questioned and worried. I can only imagine the emotions
that poured from your heart, your soul as you wrote this book.
I also want to THANK YOU for being so honest.
Parenting isn't easy.
Thank you for sharing your story

—Duana, *adoptive mom*

൪

From Half to Whole is refreshingly honest and entertaining. It is a heartfelt
and raw account of the best and worst of the adoption experience.
I LOVED IT!
I would recommend it to anyone who is considering adoption, who already has
adopted or just loves a good read. It is about the spirit of family dynamic, no
matter what the makeup.

—Beata, *adoptive mom*

൪

From Half to Whole offers a glimpse into the before and after
of adopting older children. The author has invited us to see firsthand
the ups and downs that adoptees and their families go through while becoming
a true family. Radomski has bravely offered the readers a raw and emotional
look at her family and her personal experience as she becomes a mother to two
older adopted boys from Poland. Kudos to her for taking this step! Too often
we hear only of the "before" adoption stories, not the "after" stories, and that
is truly where the real journey begins. Her documented experiences show a
mother's love and devotion and the desire to bring them together as a family.
I would highly recommend this book to anyone considering adoption.
Although experiences may vary, this book gives an excellent portrayal
of the multitude of emotions, fears and hopes prospective adoptive
parents experience and shows how the author worked tirelessly
to heal the whole family and draw them closer together.
From Half to Whole is, for Radomski, a work of the heart.

—Jimmy, *adult adoptee*

൪

This book made me feel as though I was actually a part of the experience. It was a good read filled with lots of laughs, along with the challenges that adoptive families face.

—Jeanette, *adoptive mom*

ଔ

A work long overdue that can benefit thousands of families everywhere. Finally, someone has said out loud many of the fears, stresses, and moments of uncertainty that so many deal with but never say. This book is proof that no matter how dark a situation may be, the love between parent and child can overcome regardless of the biological connection.

—Teresa, *adult adoptee*

ඩ

Your book has inspired me to keep moving forward in our pursuit of adopting a child. You went through so many struggles to make a new life for your boys, and you are succeeding! You told the truth without making it too overwhelming. The truth needed to be told!

—Christy, *prospective parent*

ଔ

Legacy of an Adopted Child

§QR

Once there were two women
Who never knew each other
One you do not remember
The other you call mother.

Two different lives shaped
To make yours one
One became your guiding star
The other became your sun.

The first gave you Life and
The second taught you to live in it
The first gave you a need for love
The second was there to give it.

One gave you a nationality
The other gave you a name
One gave you the seed of talent
The other gave you an aim.

One gave you emotions
The other calmed your fears
One saw your first sweet smile
The other dried your tears.

One gave you up
It was all that she could do
The other prayed for a child,
And God led her straight to you.

And now you ask me through the tears,
The age old questions through the years,
Heredity or Environment—which are you the product of?

Neither my darling—neither
Just two different kinds of love.

—Anonymous

Dedication

To my family and to all the families
who are considering adoption or
who have already taken that wonderful leap.

Contents

Where do I begin?

Our journey to adopt two brothers from Poland, ages five and seven, did not begin the day we decided to take this leap and end the day we brought the boys home. It started years before, with failed in-vitros and numerous emotional setbacks; with all the amazing people we met along the way who helped us before, during, and after the process; with the boys' introduction to *Amerika;* and with the upheaval it caused to all of us, which at times made us wonder if we made the right choice.

Our story is very personal and raw, but I feel people need to know about adopting older children—the effort that goes into it and the great rewards when suddenly you realize you have made it up that steep and rocky climb to become a solid family unit. Older kids need a home just like newborns and toddlers do. Yes, they are tougher, they have anger, and sometimes they have no respect for elders, because they have been terribly betrayed by the adults in their lives. But when they soften and learn to love, the rewards are great.

Is dealing with all of this easy, even if you recognize all of these issues? I find the answer very difficult to pinpoint. On one side, we have all the compassion in the world for them. We feel so badly about how they were treated so unfairly, and we feel that our love will change all of that. I wholeheartedly believe that, but in everyday life that compassion gets tested—over and over again. Moms, especially, get tested, and more sometimes than seems possible to endure. How do we get through it? With prayers, support, and more support. That strength we need must come from somewhere outside ourselves.

Of course, when we're in the midst of the daily madness, we don't always realize what our love is doing for our children. But every once in a while, when we sit back and watch them excel, watch them grow, and think about all that might have been if we didn't bring them home, it's overwhelming.

That's why I hope my boys will read this story someday—so they can understand what our life was before they came into it and how our lives changed afterward—the struggles, the anger, and the hope. Even though we fight, and fight, and fight some more, at the end of the day, we know we will love each other till the end. I recently found a letter my Dad wrote to my mom in 1939 telling her how happy he was with their recent engagement. It showed a romantic side of my dad that went on for years that we, as children, never saw or maybe never paid attention to. That's why I hope this book will give my children some understanding of us, as people and as parents, like that letter did for me all these years later.

It's hard on me when we fight for a long period of time, because it hurts me and it hurts them. I feel as if they don't appreciate the life we fought so hard to give them. They're mostly just kids being kids, but for me it's so much more than that.

Now, will your story be exactly like mine? NO. No two families have the same endings. I'm not writing this book to tell you how to do any one thing, any one specific way. I want you to know that we went into this blindly, just like you. Did we know the outcome? Did we know what we were doing *every step* of the way? Hell, NO! But life with kids, whether adopted or not, is a journey with an unknown ending. So don't be scared, don't be worried; we all go in this blindly and do our best.

Have you ever heard an adult adoptee say something like . . . "People don't understand. These *ARE* my parents; they raised me!" Those words, said aloud, can change the life of an unsuspecting child. Those are the words that finally made my husband say okay to the idea of adoption after three years of artificial insemination and in-vitro. I couldn't go on any more. I was so down and out, unable to go on with the idea of any of it anymore. Every aspect of having a baby had become so mechanical and timed. There was no pleasure anymore. The probing into our personal lives, not to mention our personal space, had become so overwhelming. But that's what we do when we are desperate; we don't care when we start out, but time takes a toll on both of you—the losses, the needles, the hundreds of vials of blood, the pain, the sonograms, the 4:00 a.m. run to New York to do the final procedures. And the hormones. Who knows what's in those hormones! If I'm not mistaken, it all gets concocted from horse urine. Oh, the fun of just knowing that!

Adoption had been in the back of my mind since I was a child. Why, I don't know, but eventually its timing was perfect. My husband was ready! The whole family—my in-laws, our brothers and sisters—embraced it with open arms. They were kind and understanding from beginning to end and still are. They are always there to talk to, to cry to, and to vent my frustrations to. They always seem to have some type of advice that does me good, and with that, we have turned out to be a pretty great family, even through the toughest of times.

Our family is now going into eight years together, and we are finally settling in. I remember reading an article once that said it takes about five years for a blended family to start to fit; I remember thinking, How the hell will I ever survive FIVE YEARS before we blend? Well, you do it. It's harder than I imagined, and I think my family will all agree with that! There are times when getting along seemed impossible. But when I hear from others what a good job we are doing and see some of the issues others have without the background of adoption, I keep fighting the fight, because others see what I don't see, and they tell me so. I'm thankful for their feedback. Without that, sometimes I don't think I would realize how good the boys are doing. That feedback encourages me to back off a little bit and take a deep breath.

Right now the teenage years are in full swing, and sometimes it seems our success is still in question and their future is still unclear. But I hope and pray that in the time we've had together, we have been able to give the boys some stability and knowledge for the future, along with security and love that will last them a lifetime.

It hasn't always been smooth and easy. Having them come to us at five and seven years old leaves a lot of unknowns for us, things we've had to face blindly, not knowing where their attitude or actions were coming from. But by being open with them about their adoption, by listening to others, and by being brave enough to confide in others, we have found answers that have brought some peace into our lives, and for that, I'm thankful. While putting our lives out there for people to judge is not easy, I feel it's necessary so that others have some realistic insight, and maybe it just might help someone. If you've just started the adoption process or you are a few years in and are questioning yourselves, whether you raise your eyebrows at us and think we're nuts or can relate and feel glad, you're not alone. I hope you enjoy this book. I also hope you get something out of it that will help you get through whatever it is you're facing or dealing with now, either at this moment or for a long time. *We all need support.* Know that until I found a support group, I had many nights crying on the bathroom floor feeling there was no one I could turn to for help. The funny thing is, they were able to tell my stress level just from the state of my hair, before I even opened my mouth. My hair was either a frizzy disaster or it was calm and in control.

Through my support group, I grew and learned. And I, along with my husband, have always found the strength to keep going, knowing that tomorrow is another day. We have never turned to any help through antidepressants or other pharmaceuticals, and for that I am proud. If you're at a turning point and don't think you can go on, know that tomorrow is another day, as is next week, next month, next year. You have the power to change things. Dig deep inside of yourself, and if you can't do it, don't do it alone. Talk about it with someone. Ideas ignite from conversations! Isolating yourself is the worst thing you can do; things build in your mind and most times are worse inside your head than they are in reality. Rely on the principles within your heart, and when it comes to school issues, confide in the principals and superintendents at your school; they are there to help. And they are great at gauging whether the trouble your child gets into is just normal kid stuff or an issue related to being adopted.

That was a huge help to me from third through fifth grade, when there was trouble—*and there was trouble!* Know you have a voice. They will listen, and if you're not getting what you want, reach out to others who are going through the same types of things. Whether it's bullying or social anxiety, Individualized Education Programs (IEPs) or the lack of one, etc., people are willing to help. At times you may feel the school system is overlooking your needs. Keep on top of them! Don't be scared to talk. Feel it out. Your conscience will guide you, and always remember: There is always someone out there who has it worse than you! Think about it, and that will put everything in perspective.

I now believe I've finally reached the point where I can honestly and wholeheartedly pour out my story—no holds barred. I'm not afraid of revealing the truth—of what the past eight and a half years have held for our family. The good times and the bad. We've been through so much.

One night while talking to my sister about the ups and downs we'd been through and the success we had even though the battles were tough at times, she said to me, "You have the battle scars to prove it." *Battle scars.* Yes, she hit it right on the head. Thus, the word "Battle scars" in the title; it says it all. Every "life" has its battlescars—some are deeper than others—and I'm sure there will be more ups and downs and roller-coaster rides that we will face even after this book is complete. But I hope to give you some encouragement to move on with your desire to adopt, because in the end—although the reasons for adoption are unique to each person—the rewards are great, for everyone involved. My boys needed a family, and we had so much love to offer. I don't regret our choice,

I've worked hard to deal with the "every-day-at-home nonsense." With *three* boys and *two* dogs, the noise level and the bickering that goes on gets to me. I can't deny that. I work very hard to stop things before they get rough, but sometimes no one hears me. So the noise level is then more intense because I am adding to it. I work on that every day. Some days I do great; other days I fail. I'm human, and so are you! Plus, that's life with kids. I'm told I will miss this when they are gone, but I doubt it. I'm looking forward to peace!

Since there are so many funny stories that have come up along the way, I want to include them here as well, to ease your fear that everything about adoption is heavy or scary. You should not be thinking about all that could go wrong before you even get your child/children. I've read a few of those books, and instead of inspiring me, I grew anxious, put the book down, and never went back to it, worried that adoption came with too much worry. Yes, the fear of the unknown is great. But educating yourself about adoption is a *must* if you are going to dive into it. It's a waste of time to read about all that could go wrong; that just made me panic *way too much*.

So I hope you enjoy this family collaboration and gain some insight on the good, the bad, and the ugly, and what we've done to get through it all while giving two children a new life that we hope and pray they will do something unbelievable with. To know we had an essential part in what they will become is something I know we, as parents, will be proud of someday. Whether they end up rich or not, we don't care, as long as they have integrity. We know we will someday embrace the fact that we took two boys out of a Polish orphanage, gave them a new opportunity, and watched them soar.

We hope that besides the laughter and the tears, our story will help you understand that no matter what you go through, from the beginning to the end of this process, you will make it! They WILL love you one day, just like any child. So as long as you can look yourself in the mirror and know you've done your best, then you've done your job right. So I leave you with this—something that I believe reveals how I felt about my parents when I was growing up. Maybe this is a little insight into the way all kids think, in general.

Now, as I reflect on what my parents meant to me, I realize I have come full circle. In my younger years, I thought they could do no wrong. I idolized them and everything they told me. By the time I was a teenager, I felt they were so old-fashioned and out of date, they couldn't possibly know anything! When I was in my thirties and married, I called them almost every day, reaching out to them for their opinions. Now, since they have passed, I wonder what they would think of who I've become and often wish that I could talk to them. I respect all their wisdom and understand exactly where they were coming from all those years. If only I knew then what I know now. . . .

January 22, 2005

In a few weeks, you, Adrian, and you, David, will be meeting us for the first time.

It's been such a long journey for us to get to this point. We've known about you since November, and learning more about you this past weekend has put a lot of fears aside for me. I just hope that for the two of you, there will be much happiness and contentment in your new lives with us.

At this point, David, you are five years old, and Adrian, you are seven. Nathan (your new brother) will be nine in three weeks. He is so looking forward to being a big brother, and I think he will do a really good job! He thinks of you every day, either by talking about you or thinking of things he wants to show you.

Dad and I also have so many things we want to show you and so much we want you both to be a part of. We hope you accept us and settle in without many problems, and I hope this transition is not scary. This is the beginning of the countdown to meeting you, and we can't wait! I think of you often when I look into the sky. I wonder what you are doing at that exact moment, and I hope you are both doing well.

I'm sure it will be a long time before you read this, but until that time, I feel I should put into words how excited we are and how we are preparing for your arrival.

We are all anxious and unsure of things, and I think that's scary for all of us. The future is so unknown! We are unknown to you, and you are unknown to us. But we have been brought together as one family, and that, we all know, is a good thing. It is something we have all wanted for a long time. So now is our time to join hands and work together to love and trust and care for one another.

Until we meet . . .

—Mom
(an excerpt from my diary, a few weeks before adopting my sons)

ೲഽൟ

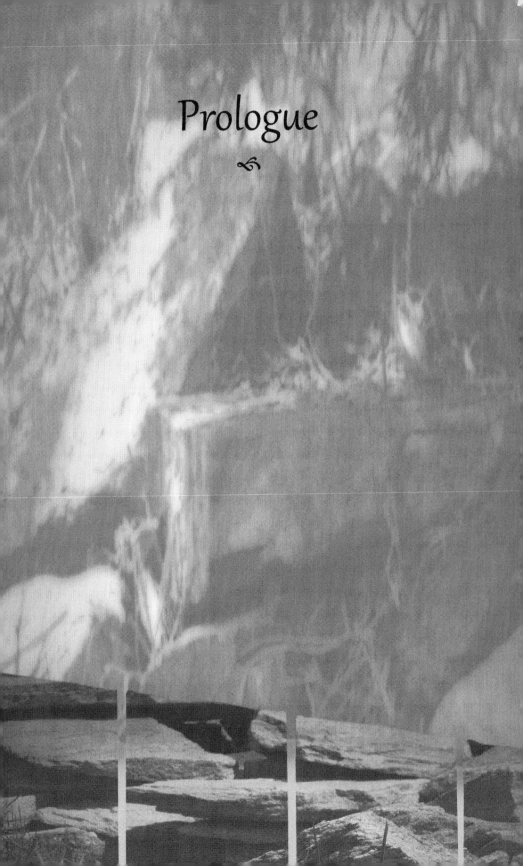

Prologue

"Ma'am, can you tell me what your son took?"
"What?" I said. "What are you talking about?"

"Ma'am, can you tell me what your son took? He tried to kill himself, and I need to know what he took."

I opened my eyes from a deep sleep to realize this man on the other end of the phone was talking to me.

April 13, 2012, was a night that started out like many others. I was lying in bed watching my favorite show, *The Big Bang Theory*, tired from the long day. It was only 10:00 p.m., but I was ready to close my eyes. Outside my door, I heard a commotion, so I opened it to see Adrian, my middle son, taping a note to my door. As soon as he saw me, he ripped it off. We'd had an argument earlier that night, so when I asked him about it, he said it was nothing. I shrugged it off and took it as some drama he was stirring up and went to bed thinking I would ask him more about it in the morning. Before long I fell into a deep, restful sleep. This was quite a change from the weeks before, when I had nightmares almost every night. A month prior, close family friends had been killed in a car accident, leaving four children behind. I had slept uneasily since then. But this night, there were to be no nightmares. On this night, my nightmare turned into reality.

At 4:45 a.m. I was awakened by Adrian as he stumbled into my room with the phone in his hand. "MOM, MOM! WAKE UP!" he yelled.

As he handed me the phone, I heard the 911 operator on the other end say, "Ma'am, listen to me. Your son tried to commit suicide. You need to tell me what he took! You need to open the front door and let the police in. Lead them to your son. If you have any dogs, please get them in a cage or outside."

In a daze, I stumbled into Adrian's room to find empty pill bottles thrown all over the floor. As I read off what he had taken, the 911 operator guided me through my thoughts and told me again to open the front door because the police and ambulance were going to be there any second. During all of this, I think I'm dreaming. Then a group of men come storming through my front door and charge upstairs toward my son's room.

At that moment, the nightmare began to unfold. Adrian had been up all night thinking about killing himself. He went on Facebook to chat with friends, telling them his plan. He wrote his suicide notes. He videotaped himself taking the pills. It appeared as though his night was long and well thought out. But it came to an abrupt halt when he panicked and called 911. Thankfully, the unthinkable did not happen.

This was all a complete surprise to everyone in the immediate and extended family. We had just been with our relatives days before, celebrating Easter. Everyone had told me that day that Adrian had been in an especially good mood. But this night was a different story; sitting on the bed with his head between his hands was a lost and lonely boy.

I knew that boy once, seven years ago, when we had first adopted Adrian. Since then, he had come such a long way, and I felt that we had done so much right. He had so much to be proud of. Now I wasn't certain our journey had been successful. The police bombarded my husband and I with all sorts of questions. With no knowledge of what had unfolded while we slept, we learned from them that Adrian had prepared five suicide notes. There was one for each of us in the family and one for his biological sister (who was adopted by another family). Each note told of his loneliness, his sadness, and how he felt unwanted. He told of times we didn't react the way he expected, and with the turn of events over the last day or two, he felt that life was not worth living.

He was mad at me for taking his phone, his computer, and all other electronics after I found out he had gotten a Facebook account without my knowledge. There was tension between us because, twenty-four hours before, I "shut him out of his world," he said. I had no sense that conversation would lead him to a suicide attempt!

As they took him to the hospital in the ambulance, my husband followed behind. I had to clean the carpet where he had thrown up and then mentally digest all that just happened. It was now about 6:00 a.m. Our two other sons were still sleeping, having never woken up through all the commotion. I had to tell them what happened and call my mother-in-law to ask her to help out for the day. The boys were mystified by the fact that Adrian would do such a thing. As David, our youngest, said, "Didn't he know he would get his privileges back in a few days?"

As the day unfolded, we worried, and searched for the root of all of this. I couldn't know then, but what seemed to Adrian to be "the end" had now seemingly become a new beginning. He now has a third chance at life with some peace within his heart that had been missing the day before his life-changing attempt at death.

How do I say that an incident like this has made him stronger and that a year and a half later it doesn't seem like the horror it started out to be? Don't get me wrong, he still has some ups and downs, but he's a teenager, after all!

Let me tell you the story from the beginning.

Chapter 1

I can't find peace; this whole situation
is wearing me down.

⤺

I'm an "at-home mom," and my husband, Bernie, is hardworking. I have always had jobs that were in the art field or the medical field, but I never really found my calling, until a few years ago, but Bernie, in my eyes, was always successful, and everything just worked for him.

Me, I struggled, never really finding my place in the working world and never really becoming the success I had hoped to be. But being a mom was the best thing I had ever come to know, and I appreciated the fact that I was able to stay home and take care of our biological son, Nathan. Yet, with that, came the price of losing myself and my self-esteem, and it rattled me to the bone. I needed to reinvent myself. Not to say that motherhood is all bad, but there are times I shake my head and say, "WOW, what am I doing this for?" At the same time, the impact I make on my kids' lives does often come back to me in a positive light, and that's when I realize it's all worth it.

Coming home with Adrian and David in 2005 was a journey that was in one way ending years of pain and suffering, but in another it was the beginning of fear and uncertainty for all of us.

Bernie and I had started our journey to have children in 1994. In 1996 Nathan, was born. Our life with him was great, and in 1999 I wanted to get pregnant again. My mom, my best friend, my father-in-law, and our beloved dog all died within five months of one another, and our world turned upside down. Losing my mom was a devastation I can't explain. We shared the same birthdays, so life without her was something I didn't think I would ever get through. Even though we had faced all this loss, Bernie and I still tried to have a child, but the cards were not falling that way. In-vitro was the way to go, we were advised, but after three years of that—the highs and lows, the exhausting treks to the doctors, the panic attacks from the sudden drop in hormones, the postpartum depression after each cycle was complete—I just couldn't go on. With the start of the Iraq war, in 2003, the news stations were telling everyone to duct-tape our vents closed in case of a "dirty bomb." I was so scared, I called Bernie at work, and he put me on speakerphone all afternoon so that I could stay calm. I feared being alone while we were attacked, so I sat by the window and waited to see the bombs come through the sky, the phone in my hand.

After each disappointing message that the pregnancy did not take, I would lie on the couch and immerse myself in my favorite comedy, *The Nanny,* so I could laugh. Since it was on three times a day, I watched it three times a day. My other escape was wishing I could be a movie star. At the time, my favorite, Jennifer Lopez, was getting engaged, and she and Ben Affleck were all over the TV. I would wish that I was her, getting my hair and makeup done, wearing the most beautiful clothes, looking beautiful, and wearing that engagement ring! I was a mess. When it came to clothes, who knew what to buy? I might be pregnant; I might not. So I went to the consignment shops to buy everything. Don't get me wrong, I got a lot of great stuff, but I didn't want to spend money on myself if I never knew if I was going to be pregnant or not. My hair? Huh, who cared what I looked like? It was too exhausting to even think of putting any makeup on.

Four years after mom died, we were now facing my father's death. My dad, a really fun guy who was always smiling and very personable, was living with us. We were enjoying our time together, but I knew time was running out, and I had to face the inevitable. At the same time, I had two more in-vitros left, and the thought of more needles was starting to be too much. I had gotten used to some of them; in fact, I had gotten so good at the needles in the stomach, I would inject myself while talking on the phone, but the final set of needles, shot into the hip, were starting to wear me down, and the loss each time of embryos was too much to bear. Having blood drawn a few times a week and having sonogram after sonogram . . . I was fading. But I was going to give it one more shot.

Oh! By the way, do you know how they teach the husbands to do these injections? They practice on oranges! One day Bernie came home from watching football with his friends and after having had a drink or two, he took an orange and started shooting it with the one-and-a-half-inch needle that was about to go into me! My hip muscles! Of course, after one try he thought he was an expert. *Oh, my God, where could I run? Where could I hide? Will I ever survive? He was going to come at ME after only practicing once on an ORANGE?* Yup, that's right, and that is exactly what happened. Oh, the pain, the black and blues. Every night for five nights I got one of those shots, one right next to the other, so the bruising was horrific. I couldn't do it anymore, but I had to try one more time. This time, though, life sent me another hurdle.

The day before I was set to start the cycles again, I was cooking potatoes in a big pot on the stove. When I went to drain them, the strainer flipped backward and the pot of boiling water hit my thigh and I got a second-degree burn from the top of my thigh to my knee.

You want to see a comedy show! I first called my neighbor Grant, who didn't quite get what I was talking about and didn't think it was an emergency, which we still laugh about today, so I then called my girlfriend, Gigi, who is a nurse. By now I couldn't think straight, and my poor son had just watched as I ripped my scalding pants off along with my skin! Gigi said she would be right over, but I knew it was a ten- to fifteen-minute drive, depending on lights. So I knew I had to think. I remembered that onions are cooling to a burn, so I peeled an onion and put it on my leg. Unfortunately, the onion was dry as a bone, so no help there! Finally, when the knock came on the door, I hobbled over to answer it, and my dog, Hunter, shot out the door like a bat out of hell and ran right pass Gigi and down the road. We started running after him but then decided the car would be a better idea. So with just a towel around my waist, we hopped in and headed down the road screaming his name. Finally we spotted him across the main street at a corner house, sitting on someone's lap in their backyard as they ate dinner. Talk about making yourself at home!

Once we got him in the car and home, we took a look at my leg. At this point the pain was unbearable and there was about thirty tiny little bubbles, which then turned into one big bubble over the next few hours. But there was no rest for the weary: The next day was needles and NYC all over again.

Now, with the burn being so close to where everything else takes place, the doctors were concerned about infection. We covered the burn with so many different things, even Ace bandages wrapped around sanitary pads. Day after day my neighbor—who is also a doctor and my best friend—and her mom, who was a nurse in the war, took care of my battered and bruised body.

Not only did I look bad, but I mentally couldn't take any more, and they knew it was now time for Murphy's Law to come into effect. I knew I couldn't go to another doctor's office, so whatever they had at home was the route I was going, no matter how unconventional it might seem. They looked at it every day, and when it was decided that the bubble should be popped, to my surprise the liquid inside came out just as hot as the water that hit my leg. *Burning!*

Well, I was a sight for sore eyes; there were needle marks on my stomach and HUGE black and blues on my hips from one end to the other. The line of the year was awarded to Bernie when he said to me (as he was shooting me with another needle), "Hon, if I didn't know you, I'd think you were a heroin addict." That night, I was leaning against the bathroom wall getting ready for another round of needles, with tears running down my eyes, biting a towel in anticipation of the pain. I was done.

Nothing had worked with any of the in-vitro attempts, from the first time when thinking they were putting in three eggs and they put in five, to the new procedures they set up to put embryos in a few days later so they would be stronger. The fear of that first attempt of five eggs was intense. All I could think of was what it would be like if those eggs split and we ended up with eight or ten kids. That night, I came home, and my friend came over, and we talked and talked about what the house would be like with all those kids. *Chaos* is all we could think about! We imagined putting all those highchairs lined up in a row in the kitchen and how it would go down. All the noise, all the crying, or all the laughing and baby noises that would echo throughout the house. It all seemed too much. The thought of all of this sent me to the couch with another panic attack. No control was all I could think about, and I was angry, because I hadn't even agreed to the five eggs or even thought about the consequences . . . Bernie told me not to worry. He said my mom was watching over me and that she would make it all okay. Well, in the end none of this came to be, and the feeling of hopelessness overwhelmed me once again.

When a cycle of in-vitro was missed because of a vacation, an off month, or anything else that prohibited us from having a chance to follow through, it meant the waiting was to continue. That waiting could turn into more than one month's wait; sometimes it would be a six-month wait, maybe even a year. Three cycles for me took three years to get through.

The in-vitro, the second-degree burn, Dad dying . . . It all was getting too much. Things for me during this time were unbearable, and the overwhelming feeling of the loss I was going through was starting to get compounded. I found myself crying quite often. Sometimes over nothing; other times a crying spell would hit over the words in a song. One day on the way to the chiropractor, I was happy, singing along with the radio in the car, sunroof open, and the sun beaming in. Within a flash it all changed. All of a sudden the tears started coming and coming. They started out slow and built up to an uncontrollable state. I got under control for only a minute while the nurse put me in a room to wait for an adjustment.

When the chiropractor walked in and said, "Hi. How are you?" the tears started all over again. He asked me what was wrong. I told him that losing my mom and my dad was hitting me out of nowhere. He so kindly said, "It's okay. I'll give you a minute." He left, and when he came back, I still couldn't stop. From there, I cried for six hours, sobbing like I never had before, but it was the last time I ever cried like that. It was hard, but it was also cleansing. Since that day, I've never gone back to that terrible state of mind. Later, realizing that I had needed to let it all out, helped to make things better. I hope that if you ever feel yourself so overcome with emotion that you lose control, you'll think back to my situation and just give into it. Let it happen. Once you're on the other side, you'll see its benefits.

What I have taken away from this . . .

Time heals everything, and crying and talking to your closest friends does more than you'll ever know. They may make you laugh, and that one moment can change everything for you.

Find a support group; lasting friendships come from the strangest places. Don't take those friendships for granted. They are there for a reason, even if it's for a brief time.

A Therapist's Insight

Messages are sent to us every day, and it is when we are open to noticing these messages that we begin to realize the path that is waiting for us. For example, pregnancy sometimes comes easily for some and seems impossible for others—either naturally or with the intervention of magical fertility treatments. Why do some women achieve pregnancy and others do not? Because there are children who enter this world, or are about to, who *need* a *parent*. And there are parents out there who want desperately to *love* a *child*. Clients that I have worked with who are adoptive parents all seem to have some things in common. One is a strong desire to be parents to a child who needs parents. Another is the determination and desire to share the love in their hearts.

Chapter 2

It's 4:00 a.m.

The embryos have died . . . again.

It is now the end of 2003, four years since this journey started. After all those years, I was filled with anger and fear. What was wrong with us? What did we do to deserve this? Why had I lost another set of embryos on my birthday, the same day that, if the last in-vitro had worked, might have been the baby's birth? Why are babies being thrown in the garbage, thrown out windows, and I can't have another one? Why is everyone else having babies and not me? At the time, I had nine friends who were pregnant, and I had to keep smiling and say I was happy for them, even though I was dying inside.

Dad's health continued to fail, so he was moved into a nursing home, and it was painful to face the truth of his decline. I had worked so hard to keep him going, which had helped for a while, but all of a sudden, he stopped progressing. He got sicker and sicker, and I knew his passing was something I would have to face sooner rather than later.

By this point I was so low, I didn't think there was any way I could climb back up. I remember sitting in the doctor's office, leg bandaged and in pain from the burn, more needles about to be poked into me and facing another in-vitro the next morning. I was fading. I recall sitting in the corner of the waiting room and not having the strength to move out of that chair. I didn't want to go home and face my dying father. I didn't want to talk to anyone. I didn't want to see anyone. I just wanted to be alone. The loneliness I felt that day was something I had never felt before, and I've never felt again. I snapped out of it, but I still can feel the exhaustion, pain, and suffering to this day. Some memories just never leave you.

A few days before his death, my father told me to really consider adopting, because there were a lot of kids out there who needed homes. That hit me hard—so much so that I persuaded my husband to come with me to an adoption conference held by *Concerned Persons for Adoption,* a non-profit organization that supports pre- and post-adoption families in New Jersey.

Bernie had a lot of fears about adoption and he needed to confront them. I was hoping the conference would help. But honestly, we were both scared. It was time for us to face the unknown. All kinds of things went through my head. We started off the day really well, with a nice breakfast, and we met some people who would eventually become a crucial part of my life in the years to come. (Little did I know then that I would one day become a part of the team who coordinates this important annual event.)

The first speaker was a woman who was adopted from Korea. She told all about her background and said these very important words: "My father died, and at the funeral someone said to me, "Well, he wasn't really your father, anyway!" Her answer to that was, "What do you mean he wasn't my father? He took care of me all my life."

At that moment our lives changed forever. Bernie leaned over to me and wrote me a note, saying, "LET'S DO IT!" Oh, my God! It was finally happening. You see, his fear was that the kids wouldn't think of him as their father. This speaker took that fear away without even knowing it. Suddenly we were on our way.

Much of the information we needed to get started was right there at our fingertips. What exciting things were we going to learn? I couldn't wait! We picked all kinds of classes, each of us taking separate classes so that we could learn as much information as possible. Bernie went off to his first class. The subject was something to do with the travel documents you needed and traveling information. I went to a seminar on how orphanage life affects the development of the child. It explained how malnutrition and lack of stimulation and intimacy causes developmental delays, oral motor dysfunction, sensory integration disorders, and auditory problems. This first class has stuck with me for years. The teacher took us on a journey in our minds of what going to an orphanage was like. As we closed our eyes, she talked us through the ride that led down dirt roads all the way up to the building that was the orphanage. Walking up the steps of the orphanage, she described the coldness of the building and the smell. And once we entered the orphanage, she told us that there were light bulbs hanging from the ceiling. Many children were inside, but the silence was astounding. By this time, anxiety was setting in. I couldn't imagine that in this day and age, these poor children are in such a horrible world. All I wanted to do was save them.

One class down, and I was moving on to the next one, hoping it would be a little lighter on the emotions. My next class focused on the health issues of children adopted abroad. They went over Hepatitis B, Hepatitis C, Syphilis, HIV, lead poisoning, parasites, malnutrition, fetal alcohol syndrome, to name a FEW. Great! Very valuable information, I thought.

Bernie entered a class on getting ready for the journey. But at the same time, I couldn't wait for lunch so I could catch my breath. I figured Bernie was feeling some of the same symptoms I was: sweaty palms, labored breathing. Maybe I'd find him running out the front door never to be seen again. Instead, we met for lunch, and he was happy and calm because, remember, he went to the light and airy seminars. I now realized that I went to the most depressing and stress-filled information-packed seminars you could fit into a morning.

While eating, we talked about what we had learned and then asked each other a question—that one question that only adoptive parents get to ask: "So what do we want, boys or girls?" I knew his answer (because he always wanted a football team), and without a breath, I knew mine. BOYS! . . . Yes, boys. I wasn't sure I could handle all the things that come with girls, like bellybutton rings or names across their asses on their low-rider sweatpants as they wiggled their hips. So in the blink of an eye, our decision was made. Yes, boys! Oh, they will run around the house and wrestle with the dogs, playing hard, loving each other . . . Yeah, BOYS!

The afternoon seminars concentrated on ways to handle an explosive child. We dove right in, now wearing the hat of prospective adoptive parents. I listened to a man tell me about attachment disorder, which affects children who had been taken away from their families, had been abused and neglected, or who had many different caregivers when they were young. This causes the children to mistrust, and they won't allow themselves to get close to anyone. It is one of the many defense mechanisms these children unfortunately have learned. He also talked about ADD, ADHD, OCD, and so on. I learned that some of these children don't respond well to conventional discipline, and it may in fact make them worse. All very important stuff! I listened intently, embracing every bit of information; I took notes; and I headed to yet another class—and so did Bernie.

By this time, I didn't want to know what class Bernie would be taking, because I was burnt out from what I'd learned but anticipated all the *good* news I would hear in *my* next class. The subject was "Understanding your child/teenager's behavior and if it is adoption or just part of growing up." Whoopee! I couldn't wait to find out what I was up against. I was terrified about the future but found the courage to move forward.

That night, on the way home, Bernie and I talked and did some game planning. We thought about the countries we would go to, and we came up with a brilliant plan: We would go to a country where we knew people so that we could stay with them. We would feel safe because they knew the country and the language. So we narrowed it down to the Czech Republic, since our brother-in-law Karel's family lived there. We could stay with them, feel safe, and get our child. What a brilliant plan! I was going to start the research ASAP.

What I have taken away from this . . .

When you are down and feel like you can't get up, stop, take a breath, and move forward one step at a time.

Don't think about forever. Keep focused on the moment, and when you feel overwhelmed, think of the words to the song *"Pick Yourself Up"* by Frank Sinatra:

"Pick yourself up, dust yourself off and start all over again."

✺

Chapter 3

Hey, Babe, I called to say I'm okay and to
see what you're up to. . . .

❧

The night we got home from the conference, I felt good that we had taken a step forward toward adoption that didn't include icing me down before a round of needles. I was in the midst of losing my dad and still feeling the pain of all the injections I had endured. This was a tough time for me, but Nathan, who was about seven, was very involved in helping. He understood, at some level, what was going on and was, as always, my rock. Even at a young age, he knew how to calm me down.

One day right after Dad died, Nathan found a play phone, (the ones toddlers pull around behind them), and he showed it to me. He then said that Grandpa was going to call us on that one day. Oh, I thought, maybe he's a little clairvoyant. I did wonder that, every once in a while, because just a week or so before, on the night my dad died, Nathan was watching TV in his room. It was a very stormy night, with thunder and lightning. Pretty scary. Bernie was out, and I was in my pajamas watching TV. Nathan came out of his room at about 7:00 p.m. and said he had a bad feeling in his belly all week and didn't know what to do about it, so we started talking.

As the conversation unfolded, he told me he really wanted to go see "Poppy." For some reason I didn't argue; we got dressed and headed out for the thirty-minute drive. When we got inside the nursing home and entered his room, I saw that my dad was lying there in a coma. As we got closer, I touched his hands, and I'll never forget how soft they were. As I spoke to him, he gently pushed me away. The nurse told me that was his way of telling me to leave him alone and to let him go; he was in his last few hours of life. I had just spoken to him the day before, and now to not be able to speak to him took me by surprise.

It's weird to say, but every time I think of that night, I visualize my dad as already being in Heaven. I feel like I could see a presence all around him. I'm happy Nathan got me to go, because my dad died a few hours later. That night has stayed with me always. One thing that truly reminds me of that time is the song "I Can Only Imagine" by Mercy Me. It helped me then, and it still helps today. When I hear it, I think of my dad walking up the cascading staircase to Heaven. It gives me absolute comfort, and I imagine that scene every time the kids and I sing this song. It is raw. Powerful. And it gives me such strength. No other song hits me the same way. Look it up on YouTube and see what I mean. Maybe it will give you strength when you need it.

The night after the adoption seminar, I went to sleep happy and content for the first time in a long time, because Bernie and I were on the same page and moving forward toward adoption.

Before I woke up the next morning, I heard a familiar voice; a voice that I knew made me happy. As I looked around, everything looked familiar to me, yet I was kind of in space. Was I dreaming? In front of me was a phone, ringing, on a table, on a piece of flooring that I happened to be standing on *IN SPACE*.

I picked up the phone, and to my surprise I heard a voice, and it said to me,

"Hey Babe."

"Dad? Is that you? . . . You died!"

He said, "I know, but I wanted to tell you I was okay. . . . What are you doing?"

"Nothing. We just got home from an adoption conference," I said.

"I know," he said. "Go for it."

When I woke up, I couldn't believe it. It WAS OH, SO REAL! And now I knew I had my father's blessing. If he came all that way to tell me to adopt, I knew I had to move forward.

So I started my research, and I quickly found out that you needed to be a resident of the Czech Republic for three years before being considered for a child, so that option was out. Then I called an organization, which from a five-minute phone call decided they wouldn't consider me yet. Their guidelines stated that I needed to grieve for six months after a loss before they would work with me.

Grieve? I had grieved more than you could know after all those years of loss and pain. I was ready to move forward, and so that phone call ended up a dead end.

From there we looked on a map to see what was close to the Czech Republic, and lo and behold, there was Poland. Perfect! Bernie's family is Polish, so we thought this was a great next option. We quickly found that you really do need to be connected with the right lawyer and agency who knows the ins and outs of the adoption scene in a specific country. So we searched a bit further and found our answer in the HR department of Bernie's job. They had access to a woman who joins families who want to adopt, with children in Poland that need adopting.

Wow! We found our answer. This made everything real, and the idea that the kids would look like us and fit into our family was a blessing for Bernie. His one stipulation through all of this was that he wanted the kids to fit into the look of our family so that there would be one less issue they would have to face on a day-to-day basis. And for me, I was okay with that because he had said yes to adoption, and since this point was important to him. I wasn't going to fight about it.

Once we made contact with the adoption agency, she would get the ball rolling. We talked on the phone. I felt comfortable with her and all that she stood for, so we were ready to move forward. It was now the beginning of 2004, and we had a lot to do: home study, fingerprints, referrals and letters from friends (just to name a few of the steps).

The referral letters, particularly, surprised me when I read them. They said things about us that were unexpected and kind. You don't really know what most people think of you—people you meet through your jobs, friends who you get to know because of your spouse. You get together with them, and once you're comfortable, you assume you have a good relationship but never truly know how much they're watching you and considering. We asked six people—friends, acquaintances, and our priest—if they would write a recommendation letter to the home-study group for us on what they thought we were like as parents and people. The letters were astounding, and with that, our confidence about getting picked rose quite a bit. One day my neighbors, Vicky and Grant, handed us their letter. Boy, did they write a beautiful letter, complete with the qualities we both had of *"LOVE, PATIENCE, KINDNESS, and STABILITY"* and how we were such *"good role models for our son Nathan."* It made me proud to read it. I thanked them, and we proceeded to sit outside at the end of our cul-de-sac on our "white trash" lawn chairs and talk, just like we did every nice night. It was a ritual we had in the beautiful weather, one I still miss dearly every sunny day since they moved.

Anyway, we were sitting there watching Nathan and her daughter ride their bikes, and an acquaintance that I had a disagreement with at the time, came over and started chatting with us about the very topic that we had recently disputed about. Right after she left, I started ranting and raving and going on and on and on. Vicky looked at me and laughed and said, "HEY! I just wrote you a referral letter saying how PATIENT and STABLE you were. Should I take that *BACK?*" We busted out laughing, and sometimes when we see each other now, we still laugh about it.

What I have taken away from this . . .

Find something spiritual to help you through your rough times. Meditation, yoga, music: They are all there to comfort you.

Believe that when someone dies, they will make contact with you; it gives great comfort just knowing it's possible.

A Therapist's Insight

Perseverance, determination, and faith are common traits that I have seen in prospective adoptive parents. These are a few of the inner qualities that I believe have given my clients the strength to achieve what they TRULY want in their lives. Most people experience some degree of fear and skepticism when they initially set out on an unknown journey, like adoption, as there are so many unknowns.

Chapter 4

Where am I going from here?

The hardest part of starting the process was facing the truth about what we would be able to handle when it came to the type of issues and disabilities we might be presented with. The sex of the child we wanted was set. Remember, Bernie wanted a football team. And I wanted *NO* bellybutton rings and *NO* names across her ass when she wiggled her hips with her low rider sweats on.

Knowing that we wanted boys, the other major decision left was whether we wanted one, two, or three children. That question took some time to digest. We needed to think long and hard. Did we want to adopt more than one child? If we did, we might be saving a family. Knowing that would be a great opportunity, should we take *that* leap of faith?

At this point, I knew I didn't want to be a caregiver the rest of my life. I was already worn out with everything I had just been through with Dad and myself. I did feel guilty that I didn't want a handicapped child. But someone said to me that we needed to be honest with ourselves, because once we were in it, we couldn't go back.

It's true; adoption is a life decision, one that can't be reversed in a few weeks. When you fill out the questionnaires, you have to be honest with yourself and your future children. Consider what you are capable of. If you feel the desire to go forward with a child with disabilities, then do that. If you sell yourself short in any way and don't do what your heart is telling you to do, you may regret it someday.

So as we sat there and wrote that we didn't want to deal with any handicaps, I took a deep breath. I accepted it because I didn't want to be overwhelmed and unable to change things once the process started.

As I contemplated our decision, I imagined what our child, our mystery child, was dealing with at this moment, at this second in his life, as we waited desperately to save him. What did he look like? Was he dirty? Was he crying? Did he have food? I remember at one point, when I was second-guessing my decision, Nathan told me that I had no right to decide "no," because we didn't know where they were and how much they needed us.

Just like the decision to not go with children from a different race, when it came to how many children we wanted, we eventually found our comfort zone as a couple, a place we felt was right for our family. We decided to put it down on paper once and for all: two boys ages three and above, with no disabilities. We hoped we could possibly keep a family together. So the time was now. We knew we might have to change our minds on some things, but in the long run we didn't change anything. Still to this day, I am happy with our decision.

As for the ages of the children, each country has their stipulation based on the ages of the parents. I was 43 years old. Poland's ruling is that the parents could not be more than 40 years older than the child. So three years old was the youngest child I could get. Also, when you are considering adoption and you have a biological child, you are told that the new child/children must not be older than the biological child so as to not mess with the birth order. That will do nothing but cause a problem for the biological child. That was another thing we needed to be aware of at decision time.

As the year went on, we continued to work our way through the adoption process, completing the FBI fingerprinting and home-study process. It took about nine months, and it was not an easy time. We started thinking about the language barrier. We started trying to figure out ways to learn Polish quickly and efficiently so that we wouldn't be dead in the water when it came time to be alone with the boys. We learned the most ridiculous ways to remember words! One year later, after studying, repeating, and writing the words over and over again, the only words I remember are Czarny (*char*-knee) which means *BLACK*. (I remembered this by picturing my knee being charred.) Czekaj (*check*-eye), which means *WAIT,* so you say it loudly! This one we got down pat because we knew it would be important in the future, and I remembered it by "checking my eye at the door." Ridiculous, right? Well, hour after hour and day after day we studied and listened. At work Bernie had a fellow employee write the words for him on his white board and quiz him. Needless to say, Bernie learned a lot more than me.

We ventured into buying a translator device for the trip, giving us some reassurance for the unknown. We thought we used it by typing in what we'd like to say and the Polish words would be spoken right from the computer. Well, to our surprise, $500 later, the machine only spit out phrases that were programmed into it in the first place, like "Where is the train?" "Where is the bathroom?". . . Nothing like "How are you feeling?" or "Do you need to go to the bathroom?"

The anguish you feel and the anticipation of it all is difficult to handle. You will think of your potential child every day, every time you have a chance to think. My only advice to get through it is to get involved with some type of adoption support group so you can talk to people who have been there and get to know people who are going through the same thing.

One such group is *Concerned Persons for Adoption (CPFA),* a volunteer support group in my area that works with those who wish to adopt. They provide educational and networking resources to those in need. Each state has its own organization, so do some research in your area. These groups are filled with people who all have something to offer each other, whether it's the chance to hold a hand, tell someone "I understand; I've been there," or on the other end of the spectrum—to just go there and let it all out on how hard it is! Someone once said to me that "adoption is not for the meek," and I couldn't agree more, but having the support you need when you are questioning yourself for whatever reason is priceless.

After we suffered and worried and talked through our waiting period of nine months, our moment came in October of 2004. I was out bowling with Nathan and some friends when I got *the call*. I answered the phone nonchalantly. *Oh, My God! They have the kids for us—Two boys, brothers that are waiting for us . . .* I was told to go home and check my email because their pictures were there waiting for us. Needless to say, we stopped bowling, called Bernie, came home, and there they were! Two kids on our computer screen from across the world. Two boys, ages five and seven, wrestling each other, one laughing and one with a mad look on his face. Let me tell you something, that picture said to me, "Oh, great, they love to wrestle. Oh, boy, rough tough boys, they will fit right in with Nathan!" Well, now I think of that picture very differently. It now says to me, "Oh boy, two boys that love to wrestle! What are we in for?"

The pictures, the wording used in the description for our kids, told us some facts about them. We were told that they both were born with normal birth weights, they both had good head circumferences and their Apgar scores were both 10s. These were all very good signs of a normal pregnancy. We were told they came to the orphanage at the ages of two years and nine months for David and Adrian came to them at five years old. David did not talk when he arrived but was developed appropriately for his age. Adrian was delayed in his development, and he needed to be calmed down and learn to trust adults. When he was fearful, he exhibited aggressive behavior until he felt safe.

I still had a lot of questions. What signs, if any, of fetal alcohol syndrome would they show? Would I be able to tell or would I miss the signs? How would they get ready for this transition? How did they get along with others, with each other? How did they get along with a mother figure? Did they listen to women or only men? Did they have siblings they were leaving behind? Did they want a new brother? *Did they want to be adopted?*

I asked these questions to the orphanage director because we had the opportunity to and had decided to accept them as ours. We were told that the older one, Adrian, got along with younger children and loved to be the center of attention. That's still rings true today. I get quite a lot of compliments on his demeanor with children. He is very, very good with kids, and yes, he does *LOVE* to be the center of attention, something that has caused all of us a lot of stress these last few years but is starting to ease. The decision that these boys were to be ours then became a reality, and before we knew it, our family had just grown in size. We were excited!

The next few months were filled with anticipation and waiting. Excited about the next few months, not knowing what we were facing, I was getting more and more nervous and apprehension was building.

Bernie was working, so he didn't have the time to think about the anxiety or fear like I did. Nathan had questions but no fear.

Even at age nine, he felt it was the right thing to do, and if I was anxious, he was there to straighten me out. One night right after we got our questions answered, things like: "How do they interact with women? Do they listen well to adults? Do they want to be part of a family with another child?" Bernie and I were lying in bed talking about the boys and how we would deal if we became afraid of them—if they became violent, for example. What if they were mad and prone to violence toward us? What would we do, and how would we feel toward them, if they punched holes in the wall? I remember to this day Bernie saying, "Love is all they need," and from that moment on, I went through a stage I call "shake and puke," because that's all I did for a week. Every time I thought about it, I shook and puked, day after day. The fear that went through me was tremendous. All the *want* I had for them turned to uncertainty. How was I going to handle all of this?

Laundry all of a sudden became an obsession with me. I was so concerned and overwhelmed with the idea of laundry for five! To this day, I can't explain it, but it was my obsession. I talked to anyone who had a lot of kids and tried to figure how they handled all that washing, day in, day out. It's all I thought about for some time—sad; when I think about it now, but you never know how you will react to change, so don't be shocked when weird, irrational fears start to overwhelm you.

As the weeks passed and the time to leave drew near, we finished up the details and we were asked to fly to Pittsburgh to meet with the adoption agency director in the U.S. and the family that was going to adopt the boys' sister. On this trip, adoption became a reality for us. We were shown more pictures, and the coordinator got to meet Nathan and see how he was handling all of this. This was to be a weekend trip and a casual way for all of us to meet, since up to this point, we had only talked on the phone. The other parents, Kim and Doug, couldn't make it out there, because there was a blizzard bearing down, so meeting them had to be postponed until we got to Poland. Needless to say, our flight there was an adventure also—so much so that I felt *GOD* as I saw Bernie coming toward me on the tarmac when I got off the plane. Let me explain. A blizzard was hitting the Northeast, and since Bernie was working in sunny Georgia, he flew to Pittsburgh from there. Nathan and I had to fly from Newark to Pittsburgh by ourselves, and Bernie would meet us at the airport.

I am a nervous flyer to begin with, and to do it with a nine-year-old on my own made me jumpy the whole time. The flight went well, but we had to grab our luggage and go down the stairs and walk to the gate from outside, and somehow Bernie got out there ahead of me and was there as I looked up. He was smiling at me, and I SWEAR I saw that glow of light that you see around God when I looked back up at him. See what stress does to you? It makes you crazy!

Anyway, the weekend went really well. The storm hit while we were there, and Nathan and I had to stay an extra day because Newark Airport was shut down. Bernie left on Sunday night for Georgia as planned, which is not something I dealt with well at that time; I always had anxiety when he left, and I couldn't show it to Nathan. I did my best, until the next morning when it was time for us to leave. There was a change in planes, and instead of taking a normal plane home, we were on a commuter flight to Ohio, then to Newark. The new plane had two propellers and looked like it held about eight people. Well, that didn't sit well; my one experience on a commuter flight was when I flew alone many years ago to Vegas to meet a friend. On that little putt-putt plane, we hit an air pocket that made the plane drop drastically, and as everyone nonchalantly read their newspapers, I let out a blood-curdling scream (no one paid any attention to me), and all I could think about was the stories my friend told me about. . . . He said there were wild boars, so if I crashed, I needed to make sure I got away from them. He, of course, thought it was *so funny,* but I don't find those things to be all that amusing! As I looked out the window, hitting the only mountain I could see and running from the wild boars was the only thing on my mind. While I sat on that plane, I felt terrified and alone.

Now I was the parent, and I needed to be in control, but I looked at Nathan and said, "I'm trying to not seem scared, but I can't do it! I'm terrified. I don't like little planes!" Bernie is always great about being on the phone with me when I have to travel. So once again he was on the other side of the line trying to calm me down, amused at my panic. Lo and behold, GOD stepped in again! Believe it or not, right when we were about to board, I heard an announcement, and our names were being called! Guess what? They changed our flight and put us on a normal plane straight from Pittsburgh to Newark, and there was peace in the world once again.

It was now January, and March 15 was set as the date for us to leave. Since everything went right that weekend for us, and the coordinator felt Nathan could handle the trip to Poland, he was allowed to come along, and so was Bernie's mom. This was something they told us wouldn't happen, because there wouldn't be enough free time, but it is something I appreciate to this day, because I feel that without the two of them there with us, I don't know if we would have gotten through everything. It was also nice to meet the woman on the other side of the phone. It made us feel more comfortable and gave us a chance to get more pictures of our new sons.

Once we came home from Pittsburgh, it was only a few weeks until we left, and that time went by very quickly. Packing was an overwhelming issue. First off, we had never been out of the country before, let alone for three weeks. Trying to consolidate three people's luggage while making sure we had everything we needed was a daunting job. There are lists of things that your agency will suggest you bring. Follow that closely and talk to others who have gone to the same country. They will know the ins and outs from experience. If they have stayed in the same hotel you are going to, that's extremely helpful. They may know if it's on a busy street, if it's in the country, what the room accommodations are, etc., and that will help you prepare. They may know a certain person at the hotel who was helpful to them that may be available to you also. They may know some place near the hotel that was a refuge for them when the kids got wild, even which restaurant may have accommodated them more than any other place in the area. This is the information I gave to a friend that was waiting to leave when I got home, and she still tells me how much my bit of information helped ease the anxieties they felt once there. She would tell herself, "If Gina got through this, so can I." You may also need shots against the known diseases of that country. That information will also be given to you from your agencies, doctors, and so forth.

I was concerned about my energy, constipation, jet lag, the food, and much more, but I also felt Poland was going to be okay. My regimen for energy was B-complex and greens. This way, constipation was under control also, and it worked. Thankfully those issues were not issues all that much. Take care and time beforehand to consider this stuff, as you will be under extreme stress during the trip, so anything you can do to help yourself, think about beforehand. Don't wait until you get there to face preventable issues. You may not speak the same language, so that will make it all that much harder.

What I have taken away from this . . .

Be real to your child. Sometimes that is the best thing you can do.

Take your time preparing for your trip. Do the best you can to prepare but know there usually is a solution once you get to your destination. If you would feel more comfortable, have family and friends help you prepare so they can be the sane one while you fall apart!

✖

A Therapist's Insight

It is always important to try and understand your adoptive or biological child's perspective. This might be the only way that parents can get a closer understanding of a child's behavior or reaction to a situation. In my professional experience as a psychotherapist, I have consistently seen a healthier and more enjoyable relationship between a child and their parent when the parent makes an effort to understand the child's view. In the case of adoption, the child's, as well as the adoptive parents' view, are usually much more complicated.

Chapter 5

I notice something new in my life—some control.

As it got closer to us leaving for Poland, I started to get excited, both because Nathan was coming with us and because we were all going to be together as a family on Easter. Easter in another country, no less!

While we prepared for the boys' arrival, life at home began to get crazy. We got a new dog (a bad idea), and we were finishing up an addition on the house, which I was tiling myself. We still had to decide on the bedroom arrangements and decorating for them, but I was confident it would all get done before they arrived. To keep myself grounded and on target for what I needed to get done, I took the photos of each of them and put them together in a small frame. I put it in the car and labeled it "My three sons."

As we finished up all the unfinished business we had to get done, I noticed something— something I hadn't noticed in years. I was getting organized, and I could finally think straight. For the first time in three years, life was coming together for me, and it was refreshing. People don't understand how life is in constant chaos when you go through all of this; it is so unsettling to feel out of control for years and years. I wondered if the boys felt this same type of unsettledness. Was losing the care and safety of the orphanage scary for them?

The day finally came for us to leave for our big trip! Bernie and Nathan went out for a little while for a fun day at Giants stadium, since our flight wasn't until 6:00 p.m. I was nervous, but that was a great way for them to start the day, knowing the next morning was the beginning of a new life for all of us.

The car showed up on time, and as we got in and started on our way, we all took a deep breath and speculated about what was to come. We all anticipated good things, and the adventure had now begun. Bernie's mom, Peggy, came with us for emotional support and to help take care of Nathan on the trip, so that alone eased a lot of tension for Bernie and me. What was waiting for us was yet to be seen. It was the beginning of the end of our year-and-a-half journey to this point—from the moment we decided on Poland to now being on our way, and what a trip it had been!

The main concern I was now having was how would we handle the orphanage when we got in there. How many kids would we see, and how many would cry for us to take them home? The whole scenario was enough to make me sick.

We made it to our flight with time to spare, and things went well on the first leg of our journey. But then we had a forty-five-minute stopover in Amsterdam, and we were 30 minutes late. That left us only fifteen minutes to get to the connecting flight on the other side of the airport. We had no idea where we were going, but we got directions and had to RUN!

This was crazy. All I kept thinking was, I hope Nathan's with us! Is he following close behind? Hope so! No time to stop! We have to get to the gate and check in! No time to go to the bathroom! Let's go!

YAY. We made it! Everyone got checked in and got down the jet way. I was finally thinking that we can relax and they won't leave without us. Suddenly, over the chatter of the passengers boarding, we overheard, "I'm so excited! I can't believe we're on our way to England!"

ENGLAND! Is that in POLAND? I don't think so! Oh, no! Turn around! RUNNNNN! We were being paged over the P.A. system. *We need to get to the right gate. Where is it? Left or right? Run runnnnn runnnnnn!!!!*

Phew! We made our transfer in Amsterdam by the skin of our teeth, and one hour later we were in Warsaw! It was morning when we arrived. We got through customs but then found out our luggage didn't make the transfer, but it was on its way, we were told. We had to pick it up later.

It finally arrived about 10:00 p.m. We received a call that there was something suspicious about our luggage, and customs wanted to inspect it. They had a concern about the locked bag. *Something suspicious?* It's only toys for the orphanage—toys I sweated over getting, wondering what would be right for them, kids who I presumed had nothing. . . . *It's only TOYS!*

Luckily, in the end we only had to open the suitcase for customs security and everything was fine, but the scare reminded me just how on edge I was.

The next morning, a meeting was set up with our lawyer. He was going to tell us about the particulars of the next three weeks: Where and how we would be getting around, a little about himself, and his role during that time. He would also fill us in with the details of our responsibilities and requirements when it came to the children, along with some background on what their situation was up to this point. We were told we were to be their "temporary legal guardians" while in the country. Paperwork was issued that explained that we would be responsible for them while we were there. That was scary, because we had to maintain their safety around this big city.

We had heard from others that we would pick the boys up every morning and bring them back to the orphanage at night. Once we dropped them off, we were expecting to have a lot of freedom. So when we were to meet the soon–to–be parents of the boys' sister, I sure hoped we'd get along! But first on the agenda was a nap for everyone. Everything went fine. The next morning, we had a meeting at the Polish Consulate to complete paperwork. This gave us custody of the boys for the few weeks we would be there with them. During our conversation with the woman who was finalizing everything, she commented that Bernie "looked just like the boys" and what a great fit it was. That made Bernie feel good.

Thankfully, we were now set to meet the kids the following day— St. Patrick's Day. Oh, the nerves. As the day went on, we found out that our meeting was being postponed one day, so we got an extra day of being our small family. Then suddenly it came to me: this choice was not only going to affect our lives, but everyone connected to us as well. Our neighbors, friends, family, school teachers, principals, the school bus drivers . . . *Everyone* who knew us and who were about to meet us, were going to be touched by our decision.

We went to dinner and had spoken to the other couple, Kim and Doug, on the phone before and planned on meeting after dinner for some coffee so that we could get acquainted.

I was told she would be wearing a lime-green poncho, so she'd be easy to spot. While enjoying our last such dinner as a threesome, I looked over my shoulder, and there was a woman in a lime-green poncho. . . . Could it be her? Would she recognize me if I said hi?

She had a picture of me that I had sent her a few weeks before— an odd one, though—but I didn't have one of them. You know us women, we hate pictures of ourselves. So I picked the only one that looked good of ME (I wasn't as concerned with Bernie). If I didn't look good, there was no sense sending it.

So the picture they had of us was one of Bernie and me. Me in my nice black silky pajamas (that's right, pajamas—*NOT* a sexy negligee), sitting on our bed. I know, you think I'm crazy. I thought I was crazy, too, but it was the only good picture of me, so that's what I sent. We still laugh about that picture when the subject comes up. Hey, if we can't do things that make us laugh to get through all the hell, what else is there? Of course, I still stick with that explanation: If I don't look good, it can't be sent.

This meeting was going to be important because it was a big part of everyone's future. There was a lot riding on this. If we didn't get along, the kids most likely wouldn't stay in touch. If it went well, we would be there for the duration supporting one another. Thankfully the latter came true.

ഇ)൫

A Father's Point of View

Nathan is a great son and best friend, but I had always felt he needed to have other siblings to complete his life. After a few years of trying and in vitro, my wife mentioned adoption, while we were on a drive. I never thought much about adoption and was very hesitant since I never wanted to be in a competition with memories of the birth parents. But my wife convinced me to go to a seminar on adoption, and I kept an open mind. After hearing an adoptive adult in her twenties speak about her life and how she felt toward her adopted parents, my hesitation disappeared. Then my wife mentioned she would like to adopt boys, and that sealed the deal. I always dreamed of coaching my kids and having them play on the same team. It was something my brother and I did not have much of an opportunity to do until later in life. So I was ready to start this adventure.

The first question was where to adopt from. I wanted to make sure the kids fit in with the family. I wanted to be in control of telling people that the kids were adopted. Plus, I wanted the kids to fit in and not be presented with that question the first time they met friends. This narrowed our search to the Czech Republic and Poland. Since my heritage was Polish, this became the final choice. For the next year, we spent a lot of time on paperwork and meetings. My impression was that it was never going to happen; everything seemed to take months to process. Then once all the paperwork was submitted, all of a sudden two twin boys were presented to us for adoption. But they were older than Nathan, and based on all the research, changing the birth order of the family was not recommended. We notified our adoption agent and feared we would never be matched again. About three months later two younger boys were presented to us, and there was no hesitation. The family was going to expand based on two short write-ups and three pictures. Amazing how a decision of such magnitude is made on a limited amount of information. So the prep and journey to Poland began.

The flight to Poland was good. I was happy my mother came along; I thought it showed us as a complete family. Plus, she could watch our son when the new brothers needed more attention. Once we arrived at the Marriott, we went down for dinner, and I felt right at home seeing a Phil Simms and Michael Jordan jersey on the wall of the restaurant. We met the lawyer the next day and started paperwork for meeting the children. Then we started the long ride to the orphanage to meet the boys.

The initial meeting was at the orphanage in a small room, and the communication was very limited, mostly thumbs-up, smiles and hand gestures. The boys were very nice, and the orphanage staff was very prepared for the meeting. I did not realize that the boys would be with us for the full few weeks. This was a bit of a surprise, since they left the orphanage with a very small amount of clothes. So off to the mall to spend money and buy clothes and they still are not officially our kids! My first challenge came in the mall when I had to speak broken Polish to the youngest as to why I could not buy him a bike. There were many more challenges to come during the next few weeks. A few I remember most: The boys were always counting, but why? Well, I tended to rotate who got to be carried on my shoulders, and they were counting to see who was on my shoulders the longest. Little did I realize the tension this was causing between them. Another challenge I faced was swimming in a non-heated pool and making sure I spent enough time with all the kids while I turned blue. And lastly, playing with a soccer ball in a bedroom (heading it back and forth over the beds) and then breaking the light! I guess I forgot the rule of no ball-playing in the house. I guess I am still a kid at heart.

The few weeks were long and tough—probably worse for the new brothers, since they did get punished a few times. When we were leaving Poland to come home, the kids went back to a different location and we had to make a decision. I was very close with Nathan and did not know if this would be the right decision for him. How could I split myself in three to be the same father to him and treat my two new sons the same way? Would it be fair to him? Well, I figured he would be the only one that could give me that answer—and he did, without hesitation. That was the moment I knew I could give the final yes in court for the adoption.

Court went smoothly, and we had to come back in three weeks to get the boys. It felt strange to leave them behind. Upon our arrival back in Poland, the boys were very excited to see us! They wondered where Nathan was, but he needed to stay home and get back to school. To come back home, I had to book two tickets to the U.S. for them. One way was very expensive, so I booked round-trip to get a slightly lower price. At this point the wallet and credit cards were exhausted from overuse. The flight home was smooth until one in-flight TV stopped working, but *a Polish-speaking flight attendant helped resolve that issue. It did seem like the right people were around at the perfect time to help us get through. I guess God knew we needed some help?*

Now, eight and a half years later, I can say with honesty there have been some great times and some bad times. They are just like most kids now. But even with all the help, they still are learning the English language. I finally got through to the youngest that he needs to tell us when he does not know a word, because I found him using the word "thing" a lot, because he was trying to hide the fact that he did not know certain words even after being here all these years. So the job of integrating the boys into society will last a long time. Looking back, it was one of the toughest decisions and most important decisions I ever made. I am proud to have done it and would do it all over again, even knowing the amount of effort it would take.

Well, back to splitting myself three ways to make sure they all get their fair amount of time and no one starts counting again!

A Son's Point of View

Once we got home from our fun afternoon at Giants stadium, I took a nap.

"It is time to wake up. We got to be at the airport in thirty minutes!" my dad yelled from the bottom of the stairs.

"Dad, I will be down in a minute. I need to get my stuff ready," I shouted back from my room, hoping they heard me from upstairs with my door closed. This whole time in my head I was just thinking, "Okay, well, they probably won't come up to my room complaining for about ten minutes, so I will sleep for five minutes and then rush the last five minutes and get downstairs before they come get me." Everyone knows that's what you say to yourself, but it never really happens.

With my eyes shut, all I heard was, "Nathan, we are supposed to be out the door! Your bags are in the car. Now get dressed and hurry up! You can eat and sleep at the airport." My dad is a freak about getting places early. The flight leaves at six, and it is still four. I have two hours, I think to myself. I didn't understand his logic, but I hurried up and got in the car as quickly as possible.

"So, are you excited to go to Poland and meet your soon-to-be new brothers?" Mom said while trying to smile but just too tired to. Tired but still jumping out of my pants, I excitedly say, "Yes!" with the most energy I had shown that whole morning. But in my mind, "Yes, going to a new country and seeing so many cool things! Who knows what my brothers will look like or be, maybe they will be famous or something!" Most people, in

general, never experience this. It is a feeling you cannot explain. I was scared that I would have no clue who these people were, and I knew I didn't know their language at all. But at the same time, I was going to another country and I may be getting two new people to live with and play with every day.

Next, we get to the airport and go through all the security that takes forever to deal with. The only thing I do during this time is look at people and see if I can find someone dressed up funny, find a food court, or just look at the sign going to the metal detector that says you can't bring tweezers or anything like that onboard and just thinking, Why?

After all that, I finally heard the non-understandable announcer that speaks their own kind of English. The one I can't understand, but somehow everyone else understands. As we board the massive plane, they have a little TV in front of every seat. This ride was nine hours, and most of that I spent watching the SpongeBob movie that had just come out, and I was so happy. After watching it about five times, I passed out and woke up to my dad telling me to put my tray up because we were close to descend! One more plane and we were there!

After we landed, we ran to our next plane and almost didn't make it! That ride was about one hour. Now I was finally in Poland, and I just want to see my new soon-to-be brothers and can't wait. We then found out we wouldn't get to see them for another few days. This was a big disappointment for me because I was already so psyched.

The next few days I had to wait at the Marriott, which had nothing but adult stuff to do, so I waited in the room and just watched *Polar Express* all day and every day. One day, my family and I had taken a trip to the amazing city of Kraków. I could not imagine how old this city was and that it was still standing and looked so nice. After this trip, it was off to a new little hotel, which became the place of some of the best moments of my life so far. After a long trip in an old van, we went to the orphanage to meet my new brothers, but at first look, this place was a ghost town. Almost every single kid that was staying there was hiding from us but would look around the corners at us like little monsters running around. I couldn't blame them. I would do the same thing if I were in their shoes. As we walked in, it was so confusing to me, because I had no clue what was happening until my family and another family came into a room with us to see the new children that our families were adopting. We were getting the two brothers, and the other family was getting their sister, and we all would be connected for life.

After our meeting, we all got back in the van and went to our new hotel. During our stay there, we did a lot, but I will get to the most important day. This day was Easter, which the people who ran the hotel made a very special day. The one waiter we had become great friends with got a bunch of eggs and actually carved them with a knife and made each of them amazing. Unfortunately, they broke by the end of the day for all of us.

That night, the hotel set up a big feast with a bunch of traditional food for all of us. It was some of the best food I had ever had! Soon after that, we found out Adrian, my new brother, had broken his ankle and my parents had to run him to the hospital. This was a long night for them, but my grandma *and I just went to sleep and saw them in the morning. A few days after this, we had to let the brothers go to a school where they would learn more about America, and the same day we took the long ride back to America, and I waited another couple of weeks till I got to see them in my country and knew they were now my brothers.*

I was very excited but also scared that they were coming home with us. I was unsure of how they were and what they would be like once they got into our house. I thought times might be tough once they started to get used to us, but they really did get tough for a quite a while. They eventually settled in, but we all knew that they needed to learn how to deal with things differently than they did in Poland. Sometimes they took it too far, but that is what most kids do, so they weren't always so different than their friends. I was happy, though, to have two brothers to help keep my days busier and to have more people in the house.

The one thing I took away from this experience as the older brother is that you have to always try to imagine yourself in their shoes. You don't know their past, but if you as a family keep trying, and if they are willing to change because of it, they may seem bad, but they can turn out good. And I think everyone deserves that chance.

Chapter 6

There they are!

Right there on the other side of that window!

After dinner we decided to meet and have dessert with our new extended family members, who were adopting the boys' sister. We knew we needed to get along, because we were in this for the long haul. Our families would be joined together tomorrow through thick and thin. This is not the norm for most adopted families; having siblings that are being separated is tough, and we knew going in we'd have to make every effort to always allow the kids to get together, talk on the phone, and whatever else in the coming years so that they never lose touch.

During our meeting, I could feel it was going to be okay for all of us. We hit it off and laughed so much about the roller-coaster ride we had all been through. While talking, we compared information and would ask each other questions. The saying of the evening became, "Let's see what the eight ball says!" They felt in many situations they had been faced with, that that was how an answer was decided, which rang true for us as well.

The next day, our family and their family piled into a van for our five-hour ride to the orphanage. Our taxi driver was a wonderful man who took very good care of us throughout our whole stay. The van was a little decrepit; it was white, with a hole right there at the bottom of my feet. Mind you, it was the middle of March in Poland, not a warm time of year, so five hours in an old van with a hole blowing constant air on my legs was not a great way to start the trip. Hour after hour we exchanged stories and started to bond, really liking each other and appreciating all we had gone through to get to this point, one of the most important days of so many lives. One of those moments that changes history. It was the here and now, and it was overwhelming.

The countryside was beautiful, I remember, but I also remember being bewildered by the site of fire after fire roaring on the sides of the roads. Where was everyone? There were no fire engines, no sirens it all seemed so surreal. Our driver didn't always understand us, so I wasn't getting an answer, and it was mind-boggling as time went on mile after mile, fire after fire. This was one of those situations where the handheld electric translator would have been useful, but I can't tell you why we didn't use it to ask the question. *"Brain Dead"* might be one explanation!

We were at the very beginning of the brain-dead stage; nothing was registering in our heads, and at the same time so many new things were happening around us. Things I couldn't grasp. Somehow we got the point across about the fires, and he told me that they were fertilizing the land and turning the crops. They would burn the earth and then sow it to get all the nutrients out. Quite an interesting idea, but I wouldn't try it in *my* yard. I'd be sure to burn down the house, the woods, and everything surrounding me!

Another startling site on our ride were the looming clouds that hung over our heads when we drove through the towns. Coal was used to heat the homes, and as the smoke rose from the chimneys, it hung right above our heads in the sky, house after house, for miles. Between all this smoke and the hole in the van, I was not breathing well or feeling very warm. The mind-boggling experiences just kept coming. Next we caught the unbelievable site of women on the sides of the roads hanging out near the entrance of the woods. They were prostitutes in short fur coats and short shorts. We never saw anyone soliciting them, but they were out there in a variety of places. It was quite disturbing, but it went along with the countryside, because down the road there was a billboard, and on it were two women lying naked on a bed, and that was an advertisement for the bed! Great selling point, I guess, but I wonder if when you buy the bed, do you get the women with it? Is it a package deal? But the best billboard was for a TV. You couldn't miss it, because inside the TV was a picture of a woman's boobs showing you her cleavage! Is that what pops up every time you turn the TV on? Or is that embedded on the TV when it's shut off? I wonder sometimes, and I have to say all these years later, along with the countryside and everything else I was introduced to on this trip, those two ads made the largest impacts and still stand out in my mind.

One last unforgettable moment was while our lawyer was driving us through town one day and we were talking. Out of the corner of my eye, I saw a sight that is engrained in my mind forever. There was a woman *crawling* up the little hill on the side of the road with *no clothes on* except for fishnet stockings and high heels. *We were in shock! Did we really just see that?* I remember asking, and to our surprise he said, "YES!"

As time went on, and we drove farther and farther away from Warsaw, which we considered "America," we knew we were getting closer to a new reality and we hoped the kids were excited.

All of a sudden, we pulled into a gated area and pulled up to a building. It was right next door to an industrial area. As he shut the van off he told us this was it, this was the orphanage. WHAT? He didn't give us any warning . . . I didn't have time to put on makeup, comb my hair . . . after all this . . . the meeting we had waited years for. I wanted to make an impression that would last a lifetime; I really felt if they didn't like me in that first few seconds, I was sunk.

I rushed to look at myself in my compact mirror so I could put on some makeup, and then I got out. At the window I saw two kids smiling at us, and waving. OH, MY GOD! There they were, right there on the other side of that window, now only a concrete wall and a window separated years of waiting for us and years of sadness and strife for the two of them. I stood there for a second and took a deep breath. Through that door was a changed life for the five of us in the car. For us, we were adding siblings to our family, and for our extended family, they were becoming parents for the first time in their lives.

As we walked in, my fear of how many kids we were going to face was becoming a reality, and I breathed a sigh of relief when we went into the main area and, to my surprise, there was no one around. All I heard was a child crying under a table off to my right. When I looked, I couldn't see anyone there, but we were quickly rushed into a back room where the boys, their sister, and the administrators of the orphanage along with our lawyer were waiting to meet us, so I never got to see who it was.

Here we go—the moment we had all waited for! Everyone was greeting us and introducing themselves. Most of the orphanage staff spoke English thankfully, so we got through all of the introductions and got a chance to look around. Remember, none of us spoke Polish, and the kids did not speak English. Honestly, a lot of it is a blur. My heart was racing and I was breaking out in a sweat. I remember my mother-in-law asking me what I thought of them as we first laid eyes on them from across the room. The two boys were in the corner giggling to each other. I don't recall where their sister was, but I remember responding that I thought they were perfect. Talking about it now, Bernie and I both remember thinking they all looked very well taken care of and that the orphanage looked clean, nice, and well-run. This was nothing like my experience at the workshop where we visualized the dirt roads and the void in the air of noise with all the children in cribs. It was such a relief!

I was shaking and telling myself to breathe, and they were just giggling and giggling. At one point as we all sat down, I looked across the room, after we had been introduced to them, and the boys were pointing at me and saying, "Momma." Bernie said he swears he heard them say, "Momma, I love you." I do remember at one point saying, "Okie dokie, Smoky," to David and he giggled, and it caught on. He loved that saying, "Okie dokie, Smoky" and so did I. It was the phrase of the year for him.

Their sister sat down next to her new mom and dad, and they were trying to make conversation. The orphanage staff was very kind to us, and our lawyer translated throughout so we were very much aware of what was going on. At one point David came over to Bernie and sat on his lap, and gave us all a once over. "What could he be thinking?" I wondered. Looking from across the room, Bernie caught a glimpse of Adrian and winked at him and gave him thumbs-up. Our first interaction with them was going well; as we were talking with the staff, they told us Adrian was not feeling all that well. He was starting to get a fever, but looking at him you couldn't tell because he had a smile from ear to ear. By the end of the night his fever spiked to 103°, but you'd never know it by his energy level. A little Tylenol and he was better by the next morning. We all sat and ate different Polish desserts as the kids drank some juice. We engaged in small talk between us and the staff; we shot video and took lots of pictures of our first moments together, and they are very special to all of us today. It gives us a great opportunity to talk about that day and to talk further about what was going on in each of our minds as this all unfolded.

After about an hour of chatting and getting to know one another, we were escorted around the orphanage and got a glimpse of their lives, their room, where they ate and played, and saw they had been well taken care of. What a relief. Hopefully, with the love we felt they had from their caretakers', we had a shot at happy children with less baggage. We took some more pictures to add to our memories, and as we did, some older kids in their teens starting coming out to see them off.

Not knowing at this point we were not ever coming back to the orphanage, we didn't get any pictures of friends so that they had these keepsakes. To this day, I'm sorry about that. We had no idea that since they had another sibling in the orphanage that was not being adopted, they could no longer have contact with them. I, for one, don't even know if their sibling was in the room with us at any point. I would've liked to have taken a picture of them all together.

As we were getting in the van to leave, it became clear to us we were in trouble. The kids only spoke Polish, and we were struggling miserably to say a few things. We could see things weren't going to go very well in the communications department.

As we started down the driveway, out the window we saw a girl, a friend we were told, holding on to the doorknob of the van crying for them to come back . . . the heart-wrenching feeling in all of us could be seen on everyone's faces.

We were off to our hotel to start our new life. David and his siblings were taking a step into the future, together, forever, and leaving this world behind them, and she, a young girl about 11 or 12, was being left behind to face the reality that she was not picked. Her friends were leaving, a dream that had not come true for her. I still wonder how she got through it.

The first separation was under way; taking them out of the only stable home they had known for three years was hard enough. But leaving their older brother behind also must have been very hard. I'm not sure what they felt about this moment. They tell us that they don't have any anger about their past. I hope they keep their peace with that forever, but time will tell.

They had to endure a second separation that day when their sister left with her family for a different hotel 40 miles away. It was decided to separate us so that there was minimal interaction between the families. They didn't want any child deciding they wanted a different parent. So off they went. We all had pits in our stomachs, and we forgot two very important things that day—things that would have made life easier for us if we had remembered. First we forgot to get the name of their hotel so we could communicate, and we also forgot to get the phone number of the taxi driver so we could go out if we ever had any free time. And as it turned out, we did have a lot of free time—way too much free time.

What I have taken away from this . . .

Things may not go as expected. Don't beat yourself up over what went wrong and what you could have done differently. Just be there for someone else when the time is right and let them know what could help them make life easier.

The moment you wait for all of your life and have anxiety about probably won't happen the way you plan it, so try not to worry. It makes life harder all the way around up until that moment.

✖

Chapter 7

Our life has begun, here and now.

෨

Soon we were entering the gates of the hotel where the adoption agency had set us up. Wow, what a beautiful place in the country. It was called The Pod, and it had a sprawling driveway that led to a beautiful resort that we would be calling home for the next two weeks. The boys were dressed in light windbreakers, and the weather was not bad for March, so we took a few minutes outside with them to take some pictures of our new family. The picture that captured the moment best is one in which they had their jackets on, with hats that had little bunny ears on top. The boys are smiling and waving from the top of a bridge that ran over the stream in front of the property. They appear to be getting along. It's a great photo; they seem so happy, and their innocence is refreshing. The first hour of our adventure is going well.

Once we were settled in our room, we went to the dining room for our first dinner together with Adrian and David. The place was empty, and the boys' wild side started to come out. Sitting at the bar, David was negotiating, I came to find out, with our translator for two cell phones. The two boys were also scheming to get some cappuccino and cigarettes and asking for steak and *frytki*—french fries. Needless to say, we were pretty clueless as to what was going on. This was just the first of many mild shocks.

We had been told that the hotel staff was aware of our situation and that they had worked with other families that stayed there from our orphanage. That was priceless, because the things that unfolded were enough to get us kicked out. The patience the staff had went beyond the call of duty, and for that I am forever grateful. The staff got us through dinner with a few compromises and quite a few explanations, both to them and to us. They were the go- between then and for the rest of the trip.

Once we got back to the room to settle in for the night, we took some pictures and got them ready for bed. When I look at those pictures, the one thing that sticks out for me is the condition of Adrian's teeth. His teeth had brown holes in some of them—holes that were very deep—so the dentist was our first adventure to face when we got home. That would be difficult, since we did not know of any Polish dentists, and we thought it would be beneficial to find one who spoke their language.

The next morning, we ventured off to have some fun and relax, spend time to get to know one another. We went to a dog show, and we took a lot of pictures of all our kids.

The beginning of our family history was unfolding, and the three boys were having fun with it, jumping on each other's shoulders and wrestling one another to get in the pictures. It was good. As we moved around the show, I noticed a woman who kept showing up everywhere we went. If we sat down, she was sitting next to us; if we went down to the show floor, there she was again. Finally I said something to our lawyer, and he told me she was a psychologist that would be following us around all day to see how everyone got along. Her report ended up being good, so I guess we passed the test.

Our next adventure was to go shopping for clothes for the boys, because they really had nothing with them, so off to the mall we went. We bought them everything, from underwear to shoes, shirts, pants, jackets, hats, gloves, soccer balls and candy. You name it, they wanted it. Three hundred dollars later they were set and ready to go. That day played out just like a movie, a movie where you see an orphan who has nothing and you watch as their entire world comes alive. It's the truth; we were living it just like in the movies!

This day was also a turning point for David and me. We were in the van coming back from the mall, and David was saying something to me, and I leaned my head backward over the seat back to listen. I looked into David's eyes and noticed the coloring. It was amazing! Blue, green and gold all blended together. As I looked at them and thought about how beautiful they were, he was looking at me upside down and noticed something, and his mood changed completely toward me. A change came over him that was so strange. I had no explanation of this change, but I had now become Mama Phewy. That's all he ever called me, and it was unsettling. He also started to punch me on a consistent basis every day. Then, about three months later, I picked him up from kindergarten, and as I put him in his car seat, his face hit my chin, and he all of a sudden raised his hands in the air very enthusiastically and yelled, "Momma WOW!"

What was that about? I thought. When we got home, he told Adrian that I wasn't growing a beard anymore, and he was SO EXCITED about that, he couldn't stand it. Years later he told me he thought only boys grew chin hair and that freaked him out knowing I might have a beard. Well, that's mighty embarrassing, but with laser hair removal, there was no more chance of a beard for me (not that it *ever* was that bad)!

§ාcՑ

AFTER THE FIRST FEW DAYS IN POLAND, the boys' "street side" started to show up. It was now the beginning of their behavioral changes, changes for me that were extremely tough.

After venturing out most days, our lawyer would leave and we would be on our own for the night. There wasn't much to do out there in the farmland. We had woods all around us, emus, chickens, swans (there was a nice pond on the property), and cows. Oh, and we had Mozart! How could I forget Mozart! He was the hotel dog.

One evening it was early yet, so we ventured off to take a walk, and everyone came—Nathan, me, Bernie, his mother, and the boys. At one point I took a picture of Bernie with David on his shoulders; everyone else was by his side. As I said, "Say cheese," David put up both his middle fingers! *What?* How did a five-year-old know this? Did it mean the same thing in Poland as it did in America? We weren't sure, so when we went back in to the hotel, we asked! YES! It means the same thing worldwide. Here we had our sweet little boy with the bunny ears the day before, now giving us not one but *two* middle fingers not even twenty-four hours later. Oh, boy! We were in for it! Today that picture makes us laugh. I have it in the scrapbook right next to the picture of them on the bridge, and it always brings up a laugh.

Palm Sunday was our third day together, and it went well, but it was a day of calamity. It started out with a ten-minute walk up the hill to this quaint church. On the way, I was getting my scarf on my neck, and out of the blue our newfound friend Mozart came up on my side, very quietly. Mozart, the hotel's dog, was a 150-pound Newfoundland. With his big size, it was amazing how quiet he was. Anyway, as he came up on the left, he ever so swiftly grabbed the corner of my scarf, pulled it off, and started running. At first he ran up the little hill on the side of the parking lot and sat there so cute with the scarf in his mouth, like a bow. But as we got close to him, he ran, and as he ran, we ran after him. Needless to say, we were a hell of a lot slower than he was!

We tried to corner him from every angle, but we were all laughing so much at times that we had to stop to catch our breath. At one point we thought we got him, because he stopped and put the scarf down. *Great, we can get it from him and get on to church! Psych!* He put the scarf down, yes, but his paw was on it, keeping it safe as he lifted his leg to pee. What? He's peeing right next to MY SCARF! As we got close, he took off, this time into the farm, running through the chickens and the cows through the manure! *Oh, my God*! My scarf! Was I ever going to get it back? We were laughing so hard we had to stop. Thankfully, as we were getting tired, someone on a bicycle from the hotel started chasing him. Who knows how it actually ended, but when I got back to the hotel, my nice fluffy, soft scarf was now lying on top of the piano in a blob—a smelly blob of mud. In the room, I washed it in the sink and worked on it for quite a while to get it back into shape. It had a hole, but I was still able to wear it. In fact, I still wear it today, and every once in a while, I'll giggle when my hand goes through the hole. That was the highlight of the day.

We did make it to church, eventually. The Mass was in Polish, so things ran completely differently than in our church. We just sat back and did what everyone else did, which wasn't too bad, but Nathan was so beat he slept right through it. The boys did well.

As time went on and our weeks in Poland unfolded, every day became a struggle. I was now being punched every day in the side of the chest (that was David's way of venting, I guess). I still don't know what that was about, but that happened day in and day out until one day I snapped! I told Bernie if he didn't get him to stop, I didn't know what I was going to do.

I was at the point where I didn't even want to get out of my pajamas. What was the use? We hardly ever had any place to go; we knew no one, and we didn't speak the language. The shows on TV were dubbed in English, but there wasn't anything that ever caught our interest. We had ONE Polish version of an American movie, and they watched that all the time unless they were being punished.

Every day, we were stuck in the hotel room with nothing to do; we had to listen, watch and hear the hell of defeat with this new concept in their little lives: VIDEO GAMES! We only had one, and we were told not to get them involved with games, but with nothing else to do for so many days, which then turned into weeks, the games were a godsend. It started out keeping them busy for the most part, but then eventually it became a sore spot, since it became the root of all evil. They found a new thing to fight about, and the song on that one game, still to this day when I hear it, sends chills through me because then and now it sounded evil.

Anyway, every day we wrote in our journal and graded the days giving them A, B, C, D or F, whatever we felt suited it. It seemed the boys did not like each other, and there were days we didn't like them very much. They seemed to be well behaved when our lawyer was around, but sometimes he wouldn't even be down the hotel driveway and the wars would begin. It seemed like they had a true hatred for each other that sometimes, I think, still comes out—not as much, but it may still be there. Sibling rivalry at its best; that's what it seemed these two lived and breathed.

As the days passed with nowhere to go and no one to vent to, the days got tougher, and the fighting got more intense. The boys were beginning to argue with each other quite often. The shame of it was, we could not understand what they were saying. The fighting was never between them and Nathan; it was always between the two of them. A lot of nights they cried themselves to sleep. We were so distraught; we would pace and wonder if we really wanted to go through with this. I remember saying one night to Bernie that backing out of this wasn't an option anymore. We had come all the way across the world, we now had them in our lives, our arms, our laps, day in and day out, talked to them about their new last name, kissed them good night every night. Now was not the time for uncertainty . . . When I was home all those months ago shakin' and pukin', that was the time to have concern! Not now! But I have to admit, the tension and exhaustion started to hit us. The pages in the journal are filled with a lot of C minuses and D's. The kids were fighting so bad they would be screaming, crying and hiding under the beds to go to sleep. At one point, Adrian took off and locked himself in the closet, another time in the men's room, and another day he ran away into the woods. We knew there were packs of dogs out there, so it was terrifying, but we found him. Understanding the boys was tough, so we were only able to make sense of things by watching their reactions to each other and by listening to the tone of their voices. If all else failed, we called someone from the hotel to help us and interpret for us.

At one point we spent the day in Krakow, and when we got back, the driver pulled us aside and said he couldn't believe what he heard them call each other. He was appalled to hear them call each other the swine of a pig. That day in Krakow, David played a trick on me that he still thinks is funny to this day. While in a restaurant eating lunch, I ordered a cup of tea. David took the opportunity to distract me by saying, "Mama, NO PHEWY, Mama WOW," and he would give me lots of little kisses on the cheek while saying it over and over again. Of course, I was laughing and saying I didn't believe this for a moment. All the while he was distracting me, he was pouring a bowl of sugar into my tea. Oh, he laughed and laughed—he just cracked himself up with that one. This was one of the rare moments I had with him, so I was trying to hold on to them with the hope that I would someday mean something to him in his eyes. So to keep me in a positive light, I would play with his little toes at night and sing, "This little piggy went to market . . . " so that I would get a laugh and maybe a hug out of him before he went to bed.

We spent day after day in Poland at the indoor pool teaching Adrian and David how to swim. The water was cold, but Bernie endured, though the fighting that would take place in the dressing room was horrific to listen to from the outside. I would pace back and forth, questioning all our efforts, all our pain, and wanted to cry, which is something I did a lot, and these types of moments made it all come to the surface. The boys hated each other, and there seemed no way to change that. As I read our journal from that time, all I see is page after page of the same words . . . Today they fought over this . . . Today this one threw a fit about . . . That one locked himself in the closet . . . Today the walls rumbled." Page after page, C minuses were at the bottom of the page, other times D's. And with the D's came the questions: Should we do this, and How do we turn back?

The hard part about all of this, looking back now, was realizing that we couldn't grasp the idea that these kids were hurting. They were losing so much, and all we thought about was all that they were gaining. Why couldn't we understand?

Why weren't they happy? Why didn't they see all the good in this? Why didn't they want to accept our love? Why couldn't they behave like normal kids? Why was everything a battle, a fight, a reason to run away? This was baffling to us. Didn't they see all we wanted to give them? We showed them pictures of our house and our extended family; we took so much time to have everything written in Polish so they would connect with us, but they weren't. They were acting out and doing so much to test us to prove that we too were going to leave them behind.

Why wouldn't we?

It's what they were used to. They wanted to prove that they didn't care if we did the same thing—they dared us to. At least, they knew their life in Poland; they didn't know what life they were coming to. When I think about it now, I understand their actions so much more. Writing this makes me look back at the situation we were in. The knowledge we all have now has opened my eyes. It saddens me that we—you, I, anyone going into this as grown-ups—couldn't handle dealing with their situations a bit better. We knew they had had a hard life; otherwise, none of us would have been there. But with all the life-changing processes we had already faced up to this point, I was worn down, so scared, so angry that things weren't going the way I'd hoped. I longed for normalcy. Normalcy is something that had not been in our life for years at this point, and I guess, for them, the same was true.

The orphanage staff would come to see us once in a while, and we would have long gut-wrenching talks with them. We were uncertain if we could stay the course, and the boys would tell them that they were trying to be good. Adrian said at one point, "I'm trying so hard to be good that I'm turning red," and David said, "This morning the devil was inside me, and now I see an angel." So we knew they were trying, but we were told they hadn't acted out this much in years.

At one point, I started to put two and two together and realized that the boys were much more immature than five- and seven-year-olds we knew back home. I couldn't compare them to how Nathan acted at their ages; I had to go back further in my memory. So one night, it hit me that the boys needed entertainment during dinner, so I bought cars, crayons and such so that they would be calm while waiting for the food, and it worked like a charm. One less issue and a few moments of peace were found in all this chaos.

Another pastime was soccer; the boys were very good but very competitive when it came to the sport. Bernie spent countless hours in the parking lot just kicking the ball and getting yelled at in Polish by David. Of course, we had no idea what he was saying to Bernie, but nonetheless, we knew he was annoyed. His tone got the point across every time. Bernie took on a lot because they liked him. David really didn't like me. (Remember, I was Mama PHEWY, and Daddy (*Tata*) was Tata WOW), and it was said with pure excitement. Adrian, on the other hand, had no issues with either of us, even though he was drawn to me, so I knew he didn't have an attachment disorder.

A few nights before Easter, we were coloring eggs. The waiters at the hotel did their best to find fun things for us to do. One of the waiters showed us how to carve a hard-boiled egg with a knife, making the most intricate designs I had ever seen. It was amazing to watch, and it is something we all still remember vividly.

While coloring eggs, we made a mess from one end of the bar to the other, and it was crazy for us, because we weren't used to being pulled three different ways. It was becoming a reality. We were outnumbered, and it was now three against two, not two against one. When it came time to clean ourselves up, David and I went into the bathroom, and for the first time since we got there, David wasn't hitting me! He was letting me pick him up and hold him up on my knee while he washed his hands. We were having such a great time. We were making lots of bubbles and splashing and laughing. That night was a first. He had even came up and gave me a kiss without any prompting from Daddy. I wondered if that moment was the beginning of change for us, and I hoped that it would be. I was longing to get along with both of these boys. I wanted to be a mom they fell in love with and hoped they felt I was there to save them, and they were happy about it. That night was a B. But it was also when we started to realize that Nathan was getting frustrated with not having Daddy all to himself. It was a natural reaction. We had been a very close family, and Nathan was the only child for nine years. Bernie started taking him out for walks alone so they could talk and bond again.

Remember, we had no car and were in the woods so we didn't have many choices on things to do. That is why you should always keep the taxi driver's phone number with you at all times. If I remember correctly, we weren't supposed to let most people know what the situation was. We also weren't free to go out and about on our own. We needed to deal with only certain people, and without that driver's number, we couldn't go anywhere, and that was hard on us. The other hardship was the fact that we didn't know anyone. Like most other couples that go through this, you're thrust into a different world in another country, and you're all alone. Thankfully, we did have Nathan and Bernie's mom with us, but at times they felt as frustrated as we did. That loneliness and longing for home really hits hard after about a week. When it hits, you wish there was someone you could talk to, someone you can just pick up the phone and call. We could have spoken to Kim and Doug, the other family, but we never thought to get the number to their hotel so that we could talk and support each other. At least now with Skype and those types of things, there are more options for keeping in touch with the outside world and your family at home.

The children's breakdowns when we were in public were hard. One such public meltdown was while at a tour of the mines. While on line, David sat on the floor with his arms crossed across his chest, crying and screaming, and then becoming dead weight when Bernie would try to pick him up. Most of the time, we had no idea why the boys were upset. We could feel onlookers watching us while we struggled to simply understand what was going on. It was tough—tougher than the normal meltdowns, because of the language barrier.

One night while in the hotel, something happened. I don't remember exactly what. All I knew was that Adrian was under the piano in the hotel restaurant (filled with people) barking like a dog. LIKE A DOG! I was mortified! Bernie was not around for some reason, so I went down there and grabbed him by the collar, got him out, and dragged him to the stairs. As we headed toward the stairs, we were struggling. We made it to the middle step, and as we wrestled, he held on to the railing with all his might, and I could feel myself losing my balance. I was so scared I was going down that wood staircase onto the ceramic tile. As I yelled for help in

English (couldn't remember the Polish word for "help" to save my life!), Bernie showed up and saved me.

A Polish man nearby looked at me and did something I never saw before. He spit in his hand, then hit the sole of his shoe and said, "Beat the living shit out of him!" I was floored! I couldn't believe it. I didn't know what to say, but I knew that I was stuck in a bad position with this kid and I was losing control. I was shaken to the bone. This was getting very real and scary for me. Was I going to have any control over these kids? How would I deal with these power struggles? I was never one to fight except when I took karate, but I was eighteen back then; now I was forty-three!

A journal entry from that time period reads like this:

"Today has been a tough day to wake up to. I don't know how it's going to turn out.

Last night was horrible. The fighting is taking a toll on us. We don't know how to deal with all of this. I feel like all of the years of pain to have a child is going to end right here, right now.

I'm trembling at the thought of this ending, you without a family for the rest of your lives and us having been through so much to get here and ending up with guilt forever. PLEASE, boys, understand this—we want you—please turn things around, and we will do our best to hang tough."

—Mom

Around this time, we were not so keen on the idea of adopting anymore, and we were continuing to question all of our efforts. At one point, we told the boys, if they didn't straighten up, they would not be coming back to America.

They were pushing all our buttons and getting in trouble. We knew they were a lot to handle at times, but we also didn't think they deserved to live in an orphanage for the rest of their lives. It saddened us and made us feel terrible. With all the days of trouble, we went back and forth with the decision of adopting. When it was time to go to bed, we were tossing and turning. We would talk, and talk, and talk. The future scared us. We didn't want to separate them, but we weren't certain if we could handle them both. The fighting between them was scary. We were torn night after night. After writing in our journal and reflecting on it all, we didn't have a solid answer.

What I have taken away from this . . .

There will be moments when you won't be able to find the words
to really convey your state of despair. At times, especially at this
point, I was feeling such pain and anguish. I know now that I had hit
rock bottom, and because of that, I couldn't see the boys' despair.
Try often to take a step back by going for a walk or doing something
that will give you a break. It will give you time to reflect on what the
children might be going through, and it may clear a path for you to see
things differently, thus being able to handle them differently.
It will be good practice for the rest of your life.

✖

A Therapist's Insight

While in the process of adopting a child, the adoptive parents are naturally experiencing many different emotions. These can range from overwhelming excitement in anticipation of being united with their child to overwhelming fear that they might not be able to bond with their child—or, that their child might not bond with them.

In the case where a child is adopted internationally and speaks a different language from the parents, there are more challenges that will be confronted—for both the child and the parents. There are even more emotional issues for the child who has been living in an orphanage. Children might not have an outlet for their feelings as they cannot verbalize them. Sometimes their fears are expressed through anger. Usually where there is fear, there is anxiety. Anxiety is about not feeling in control. Sometimes anger is the emotion that helps someone feel as if they have some control. It can also be an expression of feeling out of control and perhaps even threatened.

It is normal for adoptive parents to at times have some doubts about their decision to adopt, even after their child is living with them—especially if they are having difficulty bonding with each other or when severe emotional and/or behavioral problems become evident. Often adopted children have poor self-worth. They feel as if they are "not good enough" or are "bad," and that is why their biological parents placed them for adoption. So they might behave in ways that reinforce those negative feelings. Perhaps there is a feeling that "if I am bad enough, maybe I will be sent back to where I came from—at least it is familiar to me."

It is very important that adoptive parents interact with other adoptive parents. It is much more likely that an adoptive parent will have a better understanding of the challenges you might be facing. Only an adoptive parent knows what it feels like to be an adoptive parent.

Chapter 8

Hang on. I think we're sinking!

As Easter approached, we had some fun to look forward to. The boys' sister and her new family were coming to stay with us for the weekend. We would be spending our first Easter together as a new family. How exciting, we thought. Kim and Doug and Bernie and I got along so well, and we really felt a connection with them, one that was comforting and good.

They arrived on Saturday so the kids had all day to play, and we all had a lot of time to really get to know one another and talk. We adults talked, and talked, and talked. We had so much to vent about, so many questions, so many stories, so much we were scared about, so much we thought was hysterically funny! It was great therapy for all of us.

It rained all Saturday, so we had nowhere to go except the pool and church. In Poland the Easter baskets get blessed, and they are filled with kielbasa, a hard-boiled Easter egg, a small lamb made from butter and some bread—each item having a special meaning to the meal. Bernie and his mom walked up to the church to get everything blessed, and that was all the excitement for the day. Mozart, the hotel dog, was the entertainment for the day, and he knew it. He had so much fun with the kids; he would come in and steal their socks right off their feet. The kids would laugh, and laugh, and laugh. Mozart, he was a trip. I was amazed at how quietly he stepped. You never heard him coming.

That afternoon, Bernie and I went somewhere, and when we came back, we were told that the boys had a blast and got along really well; that surprised us until we heard why! They were on the roof off of our room (on the first floor) sweeping it in the rain and singing Polish songs really loud to no one. The video of this is hysterical; after they got done sweeping and singing, they had a fight—with the air freshener. Completely out of control, but for a few precious moments they were all truly having fun with no vicious fighting.

The next morning Easter arrived. The day was to start at 8:30 a.m. preparing for 10:00 a.m. Mass. When we went down to eat breakfast and get ready to go to church, someone in the hotel realized that night the clocks had changed to Daylight Savings Time, so we were now late for everything and couldn't make it to church. We were so disappointed, because we had nothing to do that day. We were left all alone. Except for some of the staff, there was no one even staying in the hotel. We had to fend for ourselves, and we had no one to translate for us, so we were pretty much heading into the day feeling like we were sinking before we even had a chance to swim. I was really starting to feel homesick.

Since we had bought the kids some of their first "Sunday best" clothes before we left the U.S., they looked great. We were all dressed in our Sunday best, too, so we took a lot of pictures to remember the day, but what else were we to do? All dressed up with nowhere to go. It was so depressing; I went into the ladies' room and cried my eyes out. Everything was getting to be too much. I could feel everything mounting. I just wanted to be back home with my family, sitting at Easter dinner with everyone, all twenty-six of them. Instead, we were here, in the early morning hours of Easter, in Poland, with nothing and no one to pull us through the long day that was ahead. But despite it all, I remember taking a deep breath and being thankful for the fact that we all felt safe. We had no fear of the place or the people who were taking care of us, and that to me was such a comfort.

As we sat down to start our Easter breakfast together, Bernie said a prayer, and it is one I never will forget. He said, "God, we are all together here as a family for the first time, and when you said that in hard times we will see one set of footprints in the sand because you'll be carrying us on your shoulders, I think even you are sinking because of this heavy load." You could hear a pin drop at that table, because we all felt it. We felt as if it was an unbearable load to carry, and I think some of us had tears in our eyes because we were indeed sinking. Now when I think about it, I wonder if God had stopped to get a bite to eat, like a slice of pizza, and dragged us in the sand while enjoying that little slice of heaven. Because as I write this chapter, I'm not sure if I can truly find the words to convey the state of despair we were in at that point. Had he simply forgotten about us at that moment?

As we finished up breakfast, we knew we were too late for Mass, but we all felt God understood. He knew what we were going through. So we decided to venture out to the park down the road, a ten-minute walk that would take about an hour. David decided he didn't want to go, so he threw a temper tantrum that would last almost all the way to the park. He would just stop in the middle of the street and not move, like a rock. He'd plant himself down every so often and not move. In the meantime, Adrian was so excited about the thought of a Sprite. Soda was something that was new to them. He wanted to run back to the hotel and get one. This is when we began to realize soda was a huge thing to them. Any chance they had, they'd negotiate for money and run to the soda machine by the pool and stuffed the soda bottles in the side pockets of their pants, making their pants fall down, but they would keep walking proudly down the path with their sodas. Of course, we had to set boundaries with that right away. At the same time, it was cute to watch these little guys, still so unknown to us, walking tall and proud with their pants falling down. It was something very new to them. Something they may have dreamed about having but may have never been within their reach. They were now struggling to hold on to the pants and the sodas all at once while walking down that long path to the room. It made us smile.

As Adrian sprinted his way back to the steps of the hotel to get that soda, he met up with a hole in the ground and landed right on his ankle, spraining it. Now we had David throwing a tantrum and Adrian limping and crying about his ankle. Two of us carried Adrian to the park because we were determined to get out of that hotel. And with David and his tantrums, the walk became a battle of wills. We were not going to let them win; we were going to the park because we hadn't been out of the hotel for days and days! There was no turning back. Once we got to the park, things calmed down a bit, but at one point I turned around and Adrian was gone. The boys had been playing basketball, and Dad helped David make a basket. So Adrian got furious and went running back into the fields. No one could find him for some time. Panic was setting in! We were his guardians while we were in Poland. We were supposed to take care of them; losing them was not part of the deal.

When Adrian finally walked into our sights from his adventure, he handed me a bunch of grass that I still have to this day in a vase in my office. He acted like nothing was wrong and nothing happened. It was strange to us because he was in so much pain a few minutes before, but now, miraculously, he seemed fine. How could that be? Well, come to find out, that ended up being a pattern for him for years to come. One minute he's hurt; the next he's fine.

At one point, while we were playing and swinging on the swings, Nathan needed to head back to the hotel to get something. Bernie took him back, and while walking, he got a lot of time to talk to Nathan about everything. Time that was much needed for both of them. The two of them were always inseparable, and now life was changing. Strangers were taking up Mom and Dad's time, and things weren't going so well. Nathan is very intuitive, and he saw the strain this whole thing was putting on us. But through it all, he was very understanding to both sides. He told Bernie that yes, we should still take these kids and give them a home. When hearing that, we knew we were in it for the long haul no matter how tough it got. We knew that even though they were more than a handful, they weren't bad enough to not be given a second chance.

Finally, after some time in the park, it was time to go back to the hotel. That walk back was uneventful thankfully. Adrian was limping the whole way so we decided that he should ice his ankle. We would get an Ace bandage and he would rest it. All would be right in the world again! Well! Once we got back in the hotel it was time for Easter dinner. The back dining room was set up beautifully for all of us to eat. How wonderful! The hotel chef had come in to cook for us and us alone! No other guests were in the hotel, and the dining room was closed to others. The dinner included duck, rabbit, and many other Polish delights! Right before we sat down, I thought I'd ask the bartender, who was an EMT, if there was an ice pack I could use and an Ace bandage so I could wrap Adrian's ankle and sit and enjoy dinner. He told me to hang on and he would get someone because they most likely didn't have one. The next thing we knew, while we're enjoying dinner, an ambulance arrived and the EMTs were coming to take us to the hospital! They weren't kidding, either. So we packed up and the bartender took us, following the ambulance, through the towns in the dark to the hospital.

I was actually excited! We hadn't been out of the hotel for days, and this was going to be an adventure. I had only one request on the way out, and that was from Kim. It was to "get some DIET PEPSI!"

So off we went, and after about a half hour we were at the hospital. It was dark and dreary around there. As we got inside, I remember dingy lighting and low ceilings. The nurse met us by a little room off to the side, nothing like a nurse's station in America. I remember thinking that I couldn't ever work in these conditions.

The nurse asked for the paperwork that told her his identification number for the country and that we were his guardians. After she gave the paperwork back to us, we were escorted down a long, dark hallway, and there was a homeless man lying on the floor on the way into the ER. The smell was oh, so strong! We walked past him and got Adrian to the room where the doctor was waiting. The gurney had a black garbage bag on it so he could lie down. Adrian's ankle was x-rayed, and they decided he needed a cast. Even though it was a bad sprain, the doctor told us it required a cast, not ice or an Ace bandage. So off they went to put a plaster cast on his leg. As Adrian was wheeled out to us in a wheelchair, we were given the instructions on how he was to deal with his injury for the next six weeks. "Oh, my God," I thought, "six weeks with a cast." That meant no pool for the rest of the time we were with him. It also meant he was on his own with it while we were back in America. And *lastly*, it meant that in three weeks we would have to fly home to America, ten hours on a plane, not understanding each other, with that cast on his leg. Oh, boy, things just kept getting tougher.

We knew that not being able to go in the pool was going to cause some problems, but as he came out to us in a wheelchair, he was all smiles. He was happy and said "okay" to everything with a smile, a smile we didn't trust.

That night all was okay. We found the only place open for Diet Pepsi, and it was a gas station. We found out that during Easter week all businesses are closed for the holiday. That included Easter Monday, which is called Wet Monday in Poland. A day of tradition where boys run around with water or water guns and douse the girls.

The next day, Wet Monday, we got up, and Adrian realized he couldn't go in the pool. That's when more trouble began. He wanted his cast off, not even twenty-four hours later! He was determined to get it off, so he started to cut it with a knife! He banged it into the wall by the pool so that it would break! When that didn't work, the fury came out and he was a wildman! We were in for a long week.

What I have taken away from this . . .

At times, no doubt, things will get rough. When you are going through the process, work together as a couple or as a family to care about each other and to focus on the good that is going on. Keep looking deep inside yourself and believe that God is watching you and helping you whether you can see it or not at that moment.

✴

A Therapist's Insight

We are more resilient than we think we are. People have the amazing ability to cope with the most difficult situations. How do people survive difficult situations? Perhaps people have faith that things will get better or maybe they just have the determination to turn something "bad" or "difficult" into something "good." Most often, we can get through one more day—one day at a time. Deciding to follow through on an adoption is like taking a step into an abyss—you are making a commitment to be there for your child to help guide him through his own transitions no matter what—until the day you depart this Earth.

Clients I've had who are adoptive parents have been faced with challenges in raising their adoptive child, but so have the clients who have a biological child. Challenges are faced every day by people. It really doesn't matter if adoption is a part of it or not, but with an adopted child, the transition from one stage of development to another has an added layer to it, and it can be challenging so keep searching; the answers are out there.

Chapter 9

Do we really want this?

"The last two days have been very hard. Tata (Daddy) is losing patience much easier now.... I am absolutely exhausted. This is no fun anymore.... Today, after taking away the pool privilege as a punishment for trying to take off his cast, Adrian got mad and locked himself in the bathroom again. It gets old. Our frustration is that we feel he should act more his age, but we need to remember he probably isn't seven and a half emotionally. This is tough . . . .

We can't wait to go home, but when we get home, what is life going to be like? Fits day in and day out? When we went to the orphanage, you could see Adrian was beaming; he told everyone how proud he was. Why is he willing to risk not coming to America, just for a few hours in the pool? Since starting the rewards chart, the kicking, mean words, and fighting have gotten less. David even got out of the pool today without a fight. 'Momma Phewy' has even gotten less."

—Diary entry, March 28, 2005

It's now been two days since the cast, and Bernie and I have lost our patience. The fun and anticipation of adopting was long over. We were tired of the broken promises. Adrian promised our lawyer and us that he would not argue with anyone about the pool, but he kept on relentlessly. When we punished him, he threw a fit and locked himself in the stall in the bathroom, and we had to find someone to come and talk him out of there. We even promised him *frytki* and a soda to coax him, but that didn't work. It took the bartender an hour and a half to get him out. The patience these people had for all of this was unbelievable, and I have found that to be true with every Polish person that has come into our lives throughout this whole ordeal. They all had a peace about them, even in the thick of it. Their calmness when dealing with our kids was a blessing.

We were beginning to realize that Adrian was seven and a half in years, but he was not seven and a half mentally or emotionally, and we didn't know how to handle that discrepancy. We had two more days with these kids, and we didn't know if we had the strength and stamina to continue. The days had become nothing more than going to the pool, breaking up fights, playing soccer (and getting yelled at in Polish by David for all we had done wrong with that kick, that pass— whatever you can think of), and watching out for Mozart. Most times I wasn't out of my pajamas. I was dragging mentally, physically, every which way you could imagine, and Bernie wasn't far behind. I think Nathan was doing okay and so was my mother-in-law, but we were all drained. The only thing I felt I could be happy about was that the use of "Momma Phewy" had decreased over time.

I remember one night I was walking to the dining room with Bernie holding my hand; I, of course, was in my pajama/sweatpants combo. We were walking to meet with the orphanage staff again so they could assess the situation before we were set to go back home. As we walked, I felt as if we were in slow motion, like we were in the twilight zone. We had never felt this down in our lives, and yet we were signing up to continue this FOREVER! Would we survive, and did we really want this? We were not sure. We all wanted to go home; the trip had been way more trying than we anticipated, so now with a few days left, we longed for home.

At this meeting, we learned we had to take the boys to a hospital of some sort for them to be taken care of for the next three weeks while we were home in America. That was an unexpected surprise. The children, including their sister, needed to be taken care of, someplace away from the orphanage. I think the reason being was that they didn't want anyone to influence them in the meantime—mainly, their brother. We didn't know how much this was going to cost, and who was going to foot the bill?

We left that meeting not knowing all the answers yet but knew the path they were considering. One we hadn't heard of before this time.

That night, Bernie and I were pacing the floors. Almost every night, prior to that night, when we went to bed, we tossed and turned in our sleep, asking God for answers, longing for home.

෩෨

Today we dropped the kids off at an institution for children in the mountains, about five hours away. They were good this morning, and we told Adrian that in a few weeks he would be coming to America with us. (We had been uncertain about taking both of them up to this point.) He was very excited. The boys were good at breakfast and played outside before the taxi driver came to pick us up. We stopped at the orphanage and picked up their legal guardian, then headed to the mountains. It was a long ride, and they spoke a lot with their guardian. We didn't see much of them at the institution, and we were not allowed to see their rooms. Adrian did wander off, but I kept my temper and told him it was not good what he did. The kids hugged and said good-bye. We rode home with our lawyer and their guardian and were prepped for court and found out a lot of good info on the boys.

They typically wake up at 6:30 a.m. and went to bed at 8:00 p.m. David does his homework right after school, but Adrian will try to get out of doing homework. They both ride bikes. When staff is on vacation, Adrian always helps to make all the beds and helps with the shopping; sounds like we did not see all of the boys' good qualities.

The hotel was quiet, and dinner was too. It seemed strange, but we needed the time to get a good night's sleep before court at 8:30 a.m. We watched a movie and fell asleep by 9:30 p.m.

—Diary entry, March 30, 2005

THAT NIGHT AS I WAS TRYING TO SLEEP, I thought about all we had been through—the fights, the embarrassing moments, the power struggles, the hitting. I could feel my heart racing. I was so uncertain. I wished I had someone to talk to, but everyone was sleeping. My mother-in-law was very involved, and we all knew the decision was tough. At about one o'clock in the morning, as I looked up at the moon wishing I could be Dorothy from the *Wizard of Oz* and click my heels and say, *"There's no place like home"* and be there, all of a sudden our phone rang. Who could that be? Who knew our phone number? (Up to this point we had no Internet connection, so we couldn't be in touch with anyone. We had spent three hours one night trying to email some pictures home, but they never went through.)

It was my sister and my brother-in-law calling from the States! I remember the tears in my eyes when they called. It took me by surprise, and I tear up even now when I think of it. They didn't know how important it was at that point to hear their voices. They asked us how we were handling things, and it was tough to talk about. I told them that Bernie and I were so torn. We weren't sure we wanted the boys, but we didn't want to leave them behind, either. My sister and brother-in-law made us realize that once we got home, we would have everyone's support. We would be on our own turf in America and not have all the added stresses of not knowing the language and culture at the same time.

That night had been very unsettling. Once we got off the phone, we realized we really needed to sleep because in just seven more hours we were going in front of the judge. We finally came to the conclusion that in the long run, Adrian and David didn't deserve to live in an orphanage all their lives.

℘ℭ

We went to court this morning, and things went well. Easy, not too scary. We decided on your middle names today, one is that of our lawyer, our way of honoring him. The other is that of Dad's godfather.

About 2:00 we left to go to Warsaw in order to finish up our trip, and tonight we got in around 7 p.m. and ate dinner. We had PASTA, something different for a change, and we went to bed early.

It feels weird not to have you with us, but it's nice to get back to less craziness. I know that is the thing I will crave once you come home with us. Calmness, normalcy, and consistency in your behavior.

—Diary entry, March 31, 2005

LET ME TELL YOU ABOUT OUR COURT ADVENTURE. We had an early start, picked up by our taxi driver at 7:00 a.m. Once in the car, we were off to meet our lawyer and Kim and Doug in family court. Immediately, we were brought to the hallway to wait our turn. While there, we also met with our translator. At one point before going into the courtroom, I walked to the ladies' room with our lawyer. While walking there, we ran into a woman whom he stopped and spoke with. As they spoke, I noticed that this woman looked like she had been out partying all night, and I was thinking, "God, she looks like hell." As we parted ways, I just waved good-bye as he kissed her hand and onto the ladies' room we went.

As time went on, our nerves started to kick in, and we were all kind of "shell-shocked" that we really did show up, since we were all so unsure. We laughed that Kim and Doug showed up, and they laughed that we were there, too!

While this was all going on, we didn't know that since we had been dropped off at the front door by the taxi driver, who was clueless on what court we were going to. So once he parked the cab, he ventured into this big building to find us, and when he asked where our courtroom was, he was questioned harshly about why he wanted to know and who he was. He was about to be arrested, from what he told us, because it is such a private matter.

We were now being called into the courtroom, and we were escorted to an area across from the judge's bench. The courtroom looked old, with cracked, dingy walls. Much different from American courts. We were told to stand up while the judge and another woman walked to their places. As I looked up, to my surprise, there she was! The woman from the hallway! She was our JUDGE! What a shock that was!

As court started to get under way, things got very serious and scary. I couldn't imagine what it feels like to be a criminal sitting there awaiting their fate, and I remember whispering that to Bernie as I broke out in a sweat. There was a time when we needed to stand up in front of the judge and were asked a lot of questions. With our translator by our side and questions coming from a few different people, we were asked how we would handle keeping in touch with their sister. Also what we would do if they wanted to be in touch with their sibling left behind in Poland. As court wrapped up, we learned that in just two weeks, on April 14, 2005, (Bernie's birthday) all documents would be finalized and the boys would officially be ours. The next day, we went to get their passports and brought them to the "hospital" they would stay at during our time apart.

Both families had decided to write the kids letters to tell them that we were, in fact, coming back for them in three weeks. For some reason we were unable to get in touch with anyone to get the address where they were staying. We were leaving Poland in two days and needed those letters to be mailed in Poland, not America, and we had run out of ideas! I was calling people on the way to the airport. That's how urgent I felt this all was, but in the end we never got them mailed. Once we got home, we got hold of the information and sent the letters, but unfortunately, the kids never got them. That saddened me, because even though there was uncertainty and fear on our end, we didn't want them to feel that.

Chapter 10

It's time to organize!

It's been a busy week going back to work and getting your rooms ready. Uncle Alan has been over to paint. He saw the pictures of you and is excited to be helping. Nathan's room is done and ready.

Today I thought about you a lot, and I'm starting to miss you. We spoke to the lawyer today, and he said that he has spoken to you and that you are sad and missing us. We miss you too. This time Nathan is not coming with us. This time it's just Daddy, me, and Kim. We are getting in on Sunday, the 24th of April, and we will see you on Monday, the 25th. Hope you're happy to see us!

—Diary entry, April 10, 2005

The next three weeks at home were crazy! We missed the boys more than we expected to and needed to get organized. All the while, we tried to ignore our fears. I was obsessed with the fact that I didn't know how I was going to handle all the laundry. I was asking every woman I knew with a lot of kids how they did it. I would have panic attacks about it. It's weird what sticks with you and what you become obsessed about. I was on a mission to figure out the laundry room. I wanted a system that I felt was easy and would leave things looking organized when you walked into the house through that room.

One day I went out and searched for the perfect laundry baskets, wall units that would fit and have three bins so each kid could grab and go with their clothes. I found a few things and narrowed it down to a small tower of baskets, brought them home, glad that I had finally found my solution, and showed them to Bernie. Yay! Done! *Wrong!* At that moment, all the stress of the last year and a half since we had started our venture came to a head. We had a fight, and then we both came to our senses and got down to work again. We figured everything out, and it still works to this day.

It was now time to take a deep breath and get on the plane back to Poland. This second time around, we still really questioned ourselves: *Do we really want to do this?*

So the night we arrived in Poland, we decided to go back to Old Warsaw for a nice quiet dinner for two (the last for a long time). Unfortunately, however, after we checked into the hotel, my exhaustion overwhelmed me, and all I wanted to do was sleep. It figures, right? Thankfully, after a short nap, I was ready to go, and we arrived at this great restaurant before anyone else and were seated at a beautiful table by an open window. The breeze was blowing through the screenless window with the dainty white curtains, and candles were on the table. There was no one in the restaurant except us; it was so European! Something I had never experienced before or since. It was so special. The plaza outside was quiet, not too many people around, so it was nice to be there, the two of us. It was a night I will never forget.

After our last romantic night alone, we got up the next morning and took the five-hour ride to the POD, our home away from home in Poland, where we had stayed three weeks before. We were met with the most wonderful surprise—David running to me first (not Bernie) to give a hug. He squeezed me so tight, I'll never forget, and that was priceless. We settled in there for the night because we were on the move again the next day with the boys and their sister back up to what we considered Poland's America: Warsaw.

Before we left the countryside, we said our good-byes to all the wonderful people who had taken us in and taken care of us for all that time. Then we hit the road. Leaving the countryside was hard because it was beautiful, but soon enough we were in Warsaw. When we got to the main road through the town where the orphanage was, we hit a lot of traffic. We were stuck on the top of a side street and there was nowhere to go. As we sat, the kids started to cry, but we didn't know why. As they started to carry on more and more, clawing at the windows, yelling something we didn't understand, we looked up at the driver *who could* understand them and asked what was going on. He looked back at us with tears in his eyes and said that they were crying for their grandparents, who lived down that street. *Oh, my God. We are stuck and not moving! What do we do?* There were no alternatives. For about 45 minutes those thoughts filled our heads, and we did our best not to cry ourselves. To this day as I write this, I get a pit in my stomach for the pain we felt, the pain they were faced with, and the helplessness we all faced during those tortuous moments of their final good-bye.

The next few days were chaos. We all knew time was ticking away and that our two families were about to separate forever. Even though we would be keeping in touch, we knew there was so much change about to happen. All of us were facing the biggest unknowns of our lives. I was also missing Nathan sooooo much! We got to speak with him only once during the week. I wish we knew about Skype. That might have taken away some of the stress of that week. The last night there, we met with our lawyer, and he gave us all the final details. When it was time to say our final good-byes, it all came crashing down on us. The kids were getting themselves all dolled up for their trip to "Amerika," as they called it, and having a blast. They were even writing "Amerika" on their arms in marker. I remember at one point I grabbed on to our lawyer's arm and held on for dear life, saying, "There's not going to be any more 'Jozef 911!'" That, my friends, is what we called him. When we were in need, we called "Jozef 911," and he'd be there to save us! We went on to ask what seemed to be a million questions and begged and begged to have him come to America with us.

We needed Jozef; he was our lifeline through it all—like the time he realized that David thought giving the "double middle finger" was funny. He came into the hotel room, slammed down his briefcase, and grabbed David aside and gave him a lecture of a lifetime (of course, in Polish), and that set him straight almost immediately. When we asked him how he made such an impact, he laughed but wouldn't say a thing! Things like that were priceless and comforting, knowing during our hardest times in Poland, we had someone to fall back on.

So after we left the restaurant, we all went up to our rooms to get our bearings, talk, and find strength in each other. During that time, the kids were wild. They were roughhousing, punching each other, and just totally out of control. We finally calmed them down enough to go to sleep.

In the morning we headed our separate ways, and it was tough. Once we hit the airport, anxiety mounted. We were on Continental flights home, which meant that for the next ten hours we would not have the luxury of Polish-speaking attendants! Plus, my seat and Bernie's seats were separated on the plane by about ten rows. Bernie was with David, and I was with Adrian. As we got settled on the plane, I noticed that there were movie screens on the backs of the seats, which was once again a godsend. To my dismay, ours didn't work and the plane was full, so there was no way to appease Adrian if things went badly during the long flight. There wasn't much interaction between us and Bernie and David, but Adrian and I did okay. At one point the steward came over to see what we wanted for lunch, chicken or beef. After trying to ask Adrian what he wanted and not knowing how to ask, I was lost. I explained to the steward that I couldn't speak to Adrian because I had just adopted him and we didn't speak the same language.

Low and behold, the attendant said to me, "I speak Polish." I could feel the tears well up in my eyes with happiness.

He proceeded to help me through the flight and took the kids aside and explained to them everything they needed to know once we landed and had to deal with INS. The attendant did a lot for us and really made the trip much easier.

What I have taken away from this . . .

Even in the hard times, there may be a glimmer of hope to be found if you just take a moment to recognize it. And when you do, it helps you breathe. So take that moment and hold on to it. It will last in your mind for quite a while and help you move forward.

✖

An Adopted Son's Point of View

*When I heard they were going to adopt me, I flipped out. . . .
I just couldn't wait. When I came to the U.S.A., I thought
nothing could get any better. When they showed me the inside
of their home, I was scared. I didn't really know how to speak
English back then. I also didn't really know anything about my
new parents, so I hoped when they talked to me, they would ask
a yes-or-no question. When I started speaking English, I could
understand everything they asked me.*

*I started making friends in school, and I was happy because
I could talk to them on the bus. When my parents told me what
they went through to see me and my brother, I was so happy.*

*I always called my dad "Daddy WOW" and my mom "Mama
PHEWY." I'm living the dream.*

*Coming to America was scary and difficult for me and my
brother. Leaving our family behind was super-hard, but I love
my family now. I hated the airplane the most, but having my
new family with me helped a lot. Now, eight years later, I still
think about my old family and what would happen if I stayed in
Poland and wonder what my family would be like.*

Chapter 11

A New Adventure in Amerika!

Walking up the jetway into the airport with the boys in front of us, Bernie said to me it was weird how true it was that people talk about coming to America with only the clothes on their back. We always thought they were exaggerating, but this was exactly how our boys were coming to the States—with nothing except their backpacks filled with some toys and the clothes on their backs.

Once in the airport, everything went easy, believe it or not. We took a few pictures of their first moments in America, and soon after we were on our way home.

As we drove home, the kids seemed very happy. They were singing and singing *"No, no, Amerika, Amerika, Amerika."* (For children, "no" in Polish means "yes.")

When we reached the bottom of our road, we pointed up the street and said *"dome"* (home) to the boys. It was about 4:00 p.m., and everyone in the neighborhood was out to meet us. They had balloons on the street to welcome us. David shook with excitement! He shook and shook with his mouth open, but no words came out. For about three minutes he just clenched his fists together in excitement, shook his legs, and screamed with no sound, FOR THREE MINUTES! It was hysterical.

Getting home was scary. We knew we needed a translator immediately so that she could speak for us and let the kids know what the boundaries and rules were. Thankfully, someone had recommended a woman who graciously came over that night. After going through the house and having things explained to them, the boys played and rode bikes all night. The neighbors came out with balloons to meet the boys and there was a great deal of excitement. Night One down, the rest of our life to go!

The next day, we all woke up happy but still tired. Bernie used his Polish words as much as he could throughout the day. Over the next few months, he became fluent in *dzie dobry* (good morning), *niadanie* (breakfast), *obiad* (dinner), and *dobranoc* (good night). If there was anything else we needed to explain to them, we used sign language (our make-it-up-as-you-go-along version of it, anyway). We showed them things and pointed, and we did the typical say-the-words-really-loud-and-slow-so-they-could-understand trick!

Speaking of words, one word we learned very quickly was the word *"Shushu."* It meant "bathroom" or "I have to go *NOW*!!" We still don't know the true meaning of the word, and I'm told it isn't even a true Polish word, but we do know what happened when David spit it out. Man! When that word came out of his mouth, you ran!

One of the first days we were home, Bernie and David went for a ride to the post office. Great! A nice ride out, just the two of them. What could possibly happen in that short period of time?

Well, let me tell you, while in line David said, "Tata (Daddy) *Shushu* ("I'm peeing NOW!") And before you know it, Bernie says David whipped it out and went to pee in the corner of the post office! Now mind you, Bernie was behind the velour rope and had to jump over it, scoop him up, and run out before anything came out onto the floor. He was mortified! So we now knew that *shushu* was a serious word and to not mess around when it was spoken, so we forewarned all teachers from that moment on.

As we took on the challenge of learning Polish, the words were difficult for me. It became obvious the first night we spent with the boys when Adrian had a 103° fever. He was smiling and playing as if he were fine. But when we went to bed that night, I asked him what I thought was "How are you feeling?" He smiled back enthusiastically—and told me his last name! Needless to say, my Polish went downhill from there.

So the moral of this story is, *don't* buy a translator if your kids can't read it anyway. These days you can simply use Google Translate, a free app you can download right onto your smartphone.

We soon found out they were "outdoorsy" kids, so we went to the store to buy the two of them bikes immediately. While checking out at the store, we paid for the bikes with our credit card. David later told us he thought we had stolen the bikes because we didn't use money. That made us laugh!

The boys were in their glory. They'd wake up early and fight to go outside. It didn't matter if it was raining, freezing, hot, or snowing, they were always outside. Even to this day, I catch David sometimes outside in the snow or rain playing basketball, and that's a good thing.

Since the two of them knew few boundaries, taking care of them and their needs seemed overwhelming. To start with, Adrian had major teeth problems. As I said earlier, his front teeth had brown holes, and four of his teeth on the side of his mouth from his back molar forward were rotted to the bone. So right away, the very first week here, we visited our family dentist, who then sent us to a pediatric dentist to have his teeth pulled. Luckily they were his baby teeth. To watch him suffer through that was a very tough experience for me, so I can only imagine how tough it was for him. And that was only the beginning of what was to come. But today he says he can't believe that he has such perfect teeth. Years ago in Poland he would have never imagined it to be possible.

We also had hearing problems—or so we thought. It took *three* specialists to find out he was LYING! Lying did become a big problem for him. It lasted until about the age of 14. It seemed to be his way of coping; he was a master at it. We wonder why he did it and David didn't. It was very hard to deal with, but with time and constant reprimanding, he got better. It was a tough thing. He was very hard to trust. Maybe it was a survival tactic for him, or maybe it was just immaturity. Either way, we were very frustrated with it, and it caused a lot of problems for everyone involved. The things he would pull! Sprained ankles that would miraculously disappear by the afternoon, or if he was sent to school on crutches, they would be left behind so he could slide down the banister!

We dealt with so many fake illnesses, I started to catch on that once he was told he could stay home from school, I'd wait to see how he'd react. I remember one day he was home and I had to go bowling by 9:30 in the morning, which meant I had to take him along so he would not be left home alone. As I was going into the bedroom, I caught him doing cartwheels in the hallway! I couldn't believe what I was seeing! So as I took him to "bowling," I was passing the school, and as I passed the driveway, I made a quick right straight into that driveway and brought him into the nurse and told her he was feeling much better! That was the last time that ever happened. He learned right there and then that fakin' it ain't makin' it in this house (at least in the fakin' sick department; it took years for that concept to sink in when it came to other aspects of his life, but we need to take ONE step at a time)! Nowadays, the lying has stopped, but I can't say that there still aren't situations here and there that still make us wonder.

What I have taken away from this . . .

Compassion goes only so far. When dealing with a street-smart kid who is used to conniving people, you have to learn how to always be one step ahead. I don't mean that you shouldn't believe them, but after you've been fooled a few times, it's time to show them that two can play that game.

Don't be too quick to make a decision if your child approaches you about something and you're not quite sure how to handle it. Talk to your partner first and come up with a decision together. It's okay to take an hour or two or even overnight to come up with the right solution, but make sure you are a united front. When you have time to plan, you come across much stronger and more sure of yourself.

✴

Chapter 12

The honeymoon's over . . . already?

NOTE TO THE READER: *The rest of this book recalls the past eight years at home with the boys, probably the most difficult part of this whole journey. Adjusting, learning, finding the courage to go forward, and finding the strength to know when we were wrong—it's all a part of this story. This, to me, is the hardest part of the book to write. I am nervous about how these events will come across. I'd like you to know that we work very hard every day to love and commit to our children. How we have overcome the struggles we have had, and where we have gotten the strength, is an important part of this story, as is the support and training that helped us through it all.*

When the "honeymoon" stage began to fade, the change in them really started to become apparent. Their fear and defiance started to show, and their backlash was something I wasn't expecting. It threw me for a loop, to say the least.

Before we went to Poland, we had tried to plan for the language barrier we would face once we all got home. In preparation for that, we had met with and spoken to a girl who would help us get through the summer with them. She lived in town and spoke fluent Polish. She was a wonderful asset. She would come every day and was available if there was an emergency. She helped me so much; I could never thank her enough. She spent a lot of time outside with the boys playing basketball and speaking to them. During that summer, she was able to really connect with them and learn some things about their past lives. We learned that since they were now in America and thought everyone was rich, Adrian was dreaming about us buying him a monkey, an elephant, and an orangutan. *What a hoot that was!*

The boys seemed to think that everything in America was easy to obtain, so they were thinking everything would be at their fingertips once they asked. Well, that didn't work out too well (they have since learned about chores).

The boys were very rough around the edges, as you could imagine. They got into a lot of mischief and were always on the loose. I felt as if my head were spinning when it came to watching them. Whose garages were they running into to take stuff out of? Who were they fighting with? What were they saying to the neighbors when they saw them? I know they both knew some words and concepts I wasn't too pleased with (from the little English they did know) and I was afraid who they might be saying these things to.

They were simply wild and out of control! Their moods were up and down, and there wasn't a lot of communication between us. Our translator was a big influence in changing their moods when they were out of control. The unknown of what they were feeling was tough because of the language barrier. The frustrations of not being able to get our point across, for them and for us, was there for most of the summer, but they did start to learn English within a few months.

I hated that I was always panicked and scared of what they might do. I started to see them getting mad if I spoke to another man. A big mood changer for Adrian, he tells me now, was when I hugged or kissed another child. But with the help of the translator and the help of others around me, we got through. I was hoping to start feeling like myself again. I hadn't been myself for years, and in my mind the miserable road I had been on should have been coming to an end for me. I thought that every time I went out now, I'd be back to putting on lipstick and doing my hair again—two things in my life that had gone to the wayside. I wanted to be a cool-looking, together kind of mom, one that looked good and that in turn would make them feel like they didn't end up with an old fart. I was about forty-four at the time; they were five and seven. I wanted to make a good impression on them, and I needed this for my own self-esteem; I was tired of being—and looking—run down.

I felt the hard part was behind me because the emotional roller coaster, in my mind, was over. But a new roller-coaster ride was about to begin. It turned out that every time I left the house to talk to the neighbors, go to the store, or do anything that normal life needed me to do, there were repercussions when I got home. The anger that would come to life from Adrian toward me was scary at first, but nothing I really ever felt threatened by; he would come at me like a bull in a china closet when I walked back in the house. I was taken aback by this. We had our differences, but beside the one incident on the stairs in Poland, Adrian hadn't been like this the first few months at home. I now was faced with *two* angry boys taking all their frustrations out on me. Why was this happening, and how was I to handle it? As time went on, it began to escalate. My impression of their fears was that I think their mom must have gotten dressed up, put on makeup, and gone outside to meet people. I think once she went outside, she left and didn't come back. It hasn't been confirmed, but that has always been my gut feeling.

One day our translator was at the house, so I thought I would use the time while she was there to run a few errands. Just as I was about to walk out the door, Adrian came at me full speed and rammed me in the stomach with his head. Thankfully, she was able to calm him down and get him to a place where we could at least talk some sense into him. Things like this would happen all the time and always when Bernie was out of the house. It became a daily event; the violence against me was growing. I was floored. By September of that first year, they were speaking English and the anger that we were all feeling was growing, and we could now understand each other more and more. We didn't know how to deal with each other. I was angry at the fact I hadn't gotten my life back the way I had thought I would; I was angry that David still lashed out at me every day like he did in Poland, and now Adrian was coming at me full force whenever I went out. Thankfully, I had watched Nathan grapple in his karate class for years, so I knew how to get someone into a bear hug and wrestle him to the ground. Once I got on the ground, I was on top of them holding their hands down and talking them down. This had now become a daily event. Life was spiraling out of control. Frustration and hate in me was growing.

Hate may seem like a very strong word. and I feel badly now, having worked through these issues, that these were the sentiments of our early days together. But I was furious that all this negative energy was coming out of them, directed at me, and I was upset that I saw GOOD in these kids but didn't know how to get it out of them! When I looked at them, I saw an old, worried but gentle grandfather in my five-year-old. The worry around his eyes was very present. In my seven-year old I saw such intelligence and fun. But none of this was coming through.

To this day, I still sometimes get upset when I think about all the anger and how that changed our lives and our household for a very long time, but I do realize that they were young and angry and may not have realized what they were even doing. I do forgive them, and I hope they forgive us. But sometimes it still hurts when we fight, because I feel like I am never good enough, especially to David. I hope he sees me as the woman that is here to help him grow into a man with his head held high and a good basis for life. I don't think he sees me that way. I think he tests me all the time because he sees me as someone I am not.

During all of this, I was missing an integral part of my being. Most people have their mothers there for them to call on in desperate times. I didn't have that. My mom had died in 1999, and so I didn't have her wisdom to guide me, but I did have two things she left me. The first was a conversation we had a few weeks before she died. I had called to tell her that I didn't know how I would go on without her. We shared the same birthday, and losing her was very hard. As I sat outside on that beautiful day talking to her on the phone, I imagined her on the other end withering away from pancreatic cancer, and it took all my strength to keep my composure. The whole time we spoke, she reassured me that she was okay and that she felt fine knowing that the end was near. At the same time, she told me I would be fine because I had a good man by my side. Words you never would think you'd hear from your mom. At the end of the conversation, when we said our good-byes, she hung up the phone and asked my sister, who was sitting with her, "Who was that?" That still blows my mind, because everything she said to me in that conversation was relevant, so I know those words were true to me!

The other thing she gave me was a great family for the support we would need throughout the years to come. I know that not everyone is blessed with that support. One night we were all together sitting at the dining-room table with our siblings, nieces, nephews, and in-laws, and as Bernie and I spoke about this, we got to reflect on that support and let everyone know how much they were appreciated. Their response was that they all admired what we had done and that the change in all of us was remarkable. That is something to be proud of, if I may say so myself.

In the early days of the boys' coming home, I was not whole; I was in a struggle I wasn't prepared for. We, as a *family,* were in a struggle we weren't prepared for. I thought about Nathan quite often and wondered how this would change him. Adrian and Nathan had begun fighting with each other. Adrian was determined to fight for his place in the house, and I would sit outside with my neighbors Vicki and Cathy and have to watch as they would brawl. As I watched from across my driveway, sitting in the "white trash" chairs, Vicki was on one side holding me down by one wrist, and Cathy was on the other side holding me down by the other wrist. They would talk me through these horrible scenes because we all knew, no matter how hard it was to watch, they needed to work this out.

Day after day, battles would ensue. Watching them broke my heart. Listening to them made me cringe. It was a very, very trying time. We wondered if they would ever grow out of it. We joked that they would call each other every day when they parted ways just to tell each other off. But I'm happy to say they seem to have stopped all the brawling, and the arguing is to a bare minimum now. It's much more peaceful to live in our house these days, and I'm thankful for that!

As all this fighting and unruliness was going on, I can honestly say that I was having a hard time keeping it all together. Before I left for Poland, I had joined a bowling team. It was fun to get out. I really, truly enjoyed it. It was "me" time, a time for me to connect with women my age and older. I really love older people, and at that point I didn't have too many of those types of friends around. I had moved away from my best friend, Kate, when we moved into this house, and she couldn't be replaced. Kate was in her 80s when I met her, and we spent every day together having dinner and spending time when Nathan was little, because she was alone and Bernie traveled. When she died a few days before my mom, it was hard to grasp; so connecting with these women in my bowling league meant a lot to me.

Trying to keep up with two extra boys getting ready for school added a lot of stress to the mornings, no doubt, and then having to be at the bowling alley for 9:30 a.m. was a tough adjustment. I did my best, but one day one of my teammates got annoyed with me getting there late, and she told me off. I was so shocked, because it was an outlet for me, and telling me off was just great for her, but it really hurt me and set my own spirit back a lot.

What I have taken away from this . . .

When others do not truly understand what's going on in your life,
let it go. If you know you are doing your best, that's all that matters.
Don't compare yourself to others. That's a violation against you!
Don't beat yourself up, either, when someone puts you down.
They aren't walking in your shoes.
Who's to say they would be doing any better?

✖

A Therapist's Insight

The older the child is when adopted, the more challenging the adjustment process may be. Older children may have more of an attachment to what they have come to know—hence, leaving the "home," as they knew it, or familiar people and places, can cause painful separation anxiety. The older the child, the more memories he has accumulated. Even a child who suffered abuse or neglect in his previous environment might still have difficulty leaving, because it might be all he knows. There is a sense of security that is known to us, even if it is not good. After all, the unknown might be worse than what is known.

It is important to allow your child to express his feelings and to mourn his "loss"—to cry, scream, or to be angry. Of course, this is not to say that as an adoptive parent, or any parent, you should tolerate being physically attacked by your child. If this does happen, try to not take the attack personally. This is very difficult as you want so much to love your child and for your child to love you. The challenge is to understand that your child is angry and to help him express his anger in nondestructive ways. No one likes to feel rejected—and embracing a child while he is hitting you or being mean to you is not easy, but seeking out a support system will help you and your child.

Chapter 13

School—and all that comes with it.

ༀ

Because we arrived home with the boys at the end of April and school wouldn't be ending until June, we decided that they should be enrolled in school immediately. We felt keeping them isolated from other kids at this point wouldn't be a good idea. And to be honest, I wasn't really sure how to handle them home alone, day in and day out, without Bernie home. So off to school they went, within two weeks of being in America, and things were a little hairy. They were both scared, and I was terrified. At times David would be so scared at school, he would fall to the ground in the hallway, and sob, and sob, and sob, not wanting to move. Thankfully, there was a woman who spoke Polish walking down the hall the first day. When she asked me what the problem was, I explained. She got down on her hands and knees to his level and started to speak to him in Polish, and he calmed down. Things like that happened over and over again: Polish people seemed to come out of the woodwork to help us. They got us out of many binds, and for that I am forever grateful.

Once September started rolling around and we knew that school was going to begin again soon, we were worried that we needed to get them up to speed on how to act in our society. What a challenge that was going to be—something we had no experience dealing with. Even though throughout the years our school system suspended our children quite often, it was quite fair to us and compassionate when it came to our situation.

Looking back, if we had to do it over again, we would do things a bit differently. Bernie and I both feel now that the kids needed to repeat the original grades they came here in, and we strongly suggest that to anyone dealing with this scenario. Holding the child back is beneficial to them because of the language barrier.

Their developmental age is not the same as the children they will be involved with. Not retaining Adrian caused us issues in third grade, and we also wonder if we should have held David back in kindergarten. David did so well for so long, but he has been struggling a bit the past year and a half. This year, in eighth grade, we finally made the decision to hold him back—so far, so good. He is more comfortable, he is not agitated when doing homework, and he feels much more capable than he has the last two years. It was a tough decision, but he handled it well and has matured a lot this past summer.

The two things we did do—occupational and speech therapy—were extremely helpful. Occupational therapy worked well for Adrian and his issues with personal space. He didn't know how to stay within his own space. He liked poking me in the face as often and for as long as he thought was fun. Occupational therapy also taught him how to deal with his hyperactivity. Remember, for a child without structure up to this point in his life, it is extremely hard for him to stay seated and concentrate. One thing we took away from OT that was extremely helpful for him was a "cocoon" we hung from the ceiling in the basement. It was made from a large piece of spandex, tied to and hung from a hook in the ceiling. When he sat in it, it conformed to his body and felt like a cocoon. It was something that was very soothing to Adrian, and it helped him get centered, so when he was agitated, he would sit in there. He would even do his homework in there with a flashlight. Also, we learned to put heavier blankets on him when he slept and to add some small weights to the inside pockets of his jacket. All these techniques helped him relax. It was truly amazing what we learned from his therapist and how all this worked to make his life less stressful. Another suggestion from friends was to go to a developmental pediatrician. They felt the guidance they got from these pediatricians benefited their children greatly.

Thinking back, we should have also made sure that the boys knew their address and understood that the bus drivers knew where they lived. Case in point—when Adrian was first going to an after-school homework club, he would have to take a bus home about an hour later than normal. This meant there was a different bus driver who took a different route to come home. The change freaked Adrian out, but he didn't want to tell me, so instead he would not go to homework club and would show up at home an hour early. The school would call, and he'd be in trouble. As this behavior continued, I couldn't understand what was going on. Then one day he said, "I'm afraid they don't know where I live and I won't get home." It broke my heart because I never thought of that.

Seeing their vulnerability every once in a while hit me hard. Their tough sides came through so much that we kind of forgot they could be vulnerable and get hurt. I saw this firsthand one day when David's class was planning a field trip. They had asked me to go on the class trip with them to see a play. I thought it would be a great time for us to bond. Since we seemed to have had trouble in that department up to this point, I said yes. I remember feeling good that morning and happy to be going to see a play. I hadn't done that in a long time, and since it was only going to be forty-five minutes and with kids, I thought it would be a fun and energetic afternoon. After the quick bus ride and everyone got settled in the theater, David and I took seats behind one another. This way he was with his friends and I was with the moms. I remember I was sitting next to my friend Suzy. Here we go! The play was about to start, and we were clapping for the opening scene of *Anne of Green Gables*. Now, I don't know what the whole play is really about, but the preview went something like this: This little girl named Anne Shirley becomes orphaned and is sent to an orphanage. She is then told she will be adopted by a family who owns a farm. When she gets there, she is met by a man who ends up liking her, and he tries to take care of her. When she meets his sister, she doesn't quite like Anne.

Within the scenes I hear words like, "You're no good," and "Orphans don't deserve families" . . . things like that.

Oh, my God! I couldn't breathe! My attention span for the plot was lost, and I was whispering to Suzy, and she was whispering back. We were both hoping that David and the other children in that audience that I know are adopted weren't paying attention! Forty-five minutes seemed like hours. The play was over, and I was white and scared at what I would be facing when I saw David's little face; he was only in first grade at this point, so maybe it wasn't affecting him. I can only hope.

As we left the theater, an usher said to me that she hoped I enjoyed the play. Well! I could feel the fire boiling under my skin, and I said to her that my son had just gotten out of an orphanage six months ago and that it was a horrible thing for him to see. She was speechless. But I knew it wasn't *her* fault. I felt the school should have made me aware of the storyline and prepared me for it or at least given us the choice to opt out of the trip altogether.

After we ushered all the kids onto the bus, David and I sat in a seat by ourselves, and as we settled in, I noticed he didn't sit in the seat; he curled up in a ball. I looked at him with such sadness, and I could see he was white as a ghost. The ride home was horrible and long. I didn't know what to say or what to do; my mind was racing. When I got back to school, I asked the teacher if I could take him home so that we could deal with this in private. After a few discussions back and forth trying to decide if it was better for him to finish out the school day because he may forget about it, they allowed me to take him home. In my heart I felt if I didn't get him home and comfort him immediately, I would lose him.

The car ride home was quiet, but once we got there, I knew ice cream would help heal some wounds. I thought if we cuddled in bed while we ate it, we could talk and start to heal a little bit. As I sat up in bed, he laid his head on my lap and cried all afternoon. He cried and cried, on and off for two days. Mostly he just asked, "Why?" No more than that.

I never had an answer for him, but it did make me realize how the schools dismiss the pain of adoption, the pain of not being a part of this family's tree, and how much it hurts when it hits home and you are faced with no solid answers for the hurting child.

Fast-forward a few months, into the next school year. On the other side of the fence, we had a different school issue raise its ugly face. Within the first two weeks of school I got a call that Adrian hit a kid on the bus and told him to "Fuck off." *GREAT!* He doesn't know a lot of English, but he knows that? Anyway, I was told I needed to meet with the other child's parent at 8:00 a.m. the next morning in the principal's office. So there I went, all by myself, not good at confrontation and terrified at what I was going to face. I have never been in this situation before because Nathan never caused much trouble. I was learning that life, for us, was drastically taking on a whole new twist.

Next morning I arrive at 8:00 a.m. You can imagine the tension in the room! You could cut it with a knife. The mom is furious and telling me that if it were to happen again, she would allow her son to beat my son up and wouldn't have any problem with that. As I sat there, I was worried about what to say or do. She didn't know our situation, and I was concerned about telling her. I looked at the principal and asked him what he thought I should do, and he said, "Go with your gut." So that's what I did. I explained our situation, and she backed off, and that's what I have found most people did.

Over the years, we've had countless times when the boys were in trouble at school. Their social skills left a lot to be desired. They were getting into fights and doing things that were inappropriate on a weekly basis—things I just couldn't begin to deal with. But I have to say, people were very supportive of us and took me aside and talked to me sometimes for hours to help me cope.

Another side that came out that we still laugh about to this day is the change in food and what it did to their stomachs. The smells that would be brewing inside them were horrendous! Once that "witch's brew" hit the light of day, people would literally leave the room. During that time, we were in the karate waiting room quite often, and the two of them would either be beating each other up or letting that brew rip, and people would run. It was mortifying for them. I remember one day David came home from school and said he wanted to put an air freshener in his pants to mask the smell. *So many* things were tough in many different ways.

How did Bernie handle all of this? He was less frazzled than I was, partly because he was at work much of the time and I was home day in and day out with the kids. I called him at work quite often because of all of the brawling, fighting, screaming, and carrying on. I know I was guilty of unnecessary screaming and yelling in those days. I remember screaming so much and while doing it saying to myself, *What's going on? Calm down. Don't yell like that. What happened to you? How could you be so out of control? Don't scream so loud!* But I couldn't stop it. I could feel the blood vessels about to burst inside my neck. It took years to finally learn control, but eventually I did.

Control, or the start of it, came to me by way of an old friend. One day I was at a conference and we were talking about kids, as all mothers do, and she asked me how I was doing. As I proceeded to tell her how out of control I was feeling, she told me about a program she had used with her son, a program that I had heard about on the radio and seen many, many times on TV but never thought to consider it. The name of the program is *Total Transformation*, and I can tell you it has changed our lives. It has taught me that I don't need to be invited into all the fights that go on around me. I have learned to sit down with eight specific steps to solve problems, helping the kids come up with their own solutions to the problems, and it has been very good. Having them sit down and write out the solutions to what they should do next time they are faced with the issue has really helped them grow, and with that, the household has changed drastically for the better. In addition, it helps to teach them that they are responsible for their actions and for the outcome. Along with that it helps them with solving problems. The founder of the program, James Lehman, explains that without this knowledge of solving problems, children may be more prone to try to commit suicide. It seems to be a leading cause of suicide attempts, more than depression.

I think these strategies really helped the kids with the ADHD everyone labeled them with. I truly believe my kids didn't and *don't* have it. For years I fought not to have Adrian labeled, because being adopted at an older age, they had never learned the structure of school and life that we take for granted. They weren't used to sitting in a classroom, paying attention, and interacting with other kids in the right way. They were frustrated, behind in comprehension, and not used to our world. And for those reasons, I didn't feel it was right to label him. Their background spoke volumes to me, and it told me Adrian didn't need medication to right this problem. But I then gave in. I learned that this label would get him help in school, whether I medicated him or not. Our decision was not to medicate and to teach strategies. I feel this has been the right path, and there is not a day that goes by that I regret our decision. It is easy to label. It's definitely easier to medicate, but we stuck it out, and with persistence he is doing better. We did opt for an alternative method of vitamins, one that is very helpful and with no side effects. I give both boys a vitamin called Vitamind, which helps with focus. I like that this has nothing in it that can harm them when they are on it or if they don't take it. Another part of this was a concern for lead. I had been told that lead could also cause symptoms of ADD, so I had a hair test done on Adrian and it came up positive (in the high range), for 6 out of 9 toxic elements. It also showed he was low in 4 out of 11 nutrient elements. Through a process of detoxing his body, and the right food and supplements, he is now fine.

Then one day I was watching a show and they were talking about feng shui. A woman proceeded to talk about how her daughter was always in turmoil. Wow, that sounded familiar! They explained that if a person's bed is situated over the stove and/or oven, the energy under them is fire, and it keeps them unsettled. If you move them to a firm wall and above the coolness of the refrigerator, they will be more peaceful. You know, I have to say it worked. We changed his room around a few months ago with a new bed and put it over the refrigerator. We have noticed that he is thinking more before he acts and is more settled when he sleeps. Who knew?

What I have taken away from this . . .

Trust others to help you through.
Many great ideas come from talking and confiding in others.

People have a different perspective when they are not involved. Also when your child is first in school and has a change to the normal routine, let them know you have taken care of getting them home safely.

✱

Chapter 14

"I never thought people would miss me. . . ."

In 2012 Adrian turned fourteen, and we saw huge changes in him for the better. He was doing better in school, and he wasn't losing his homework like he had in the past. The amount of trouble he was getting into was going down. He had done really well that year in football also. On Easter Sunday his trainer called us to say he thought Adrian had strong potential to be a great football player if he put his mind to it. When that call came in, all Adrian heard was Bernie's side of the conversation, which wasn't much, because he was just listening. Adrian was nervous. He thought he was in trouble for something, but once Bernie got off the phone and told him the good news, he was so happy.

"Wow," we thought, "things are really looking up for him." He had worked hard to change; his bad reputation was starting to disappear. The only things that we were concerned with at this point were the dreams he told me he was having and the fact that, like all of us, he was sad over the death of our close friends, Carol and Stan, who had recently been killed in a car accident.

He had just started opening up to me about this dream, and I had just, for the first time, witnessed him actually having it. It was a wild scene: He was actually running sideways in his bed while still lying there. Does that make any sense? He then stood up, flipped himself around, and slammed his body into his bed. His breathing was very fast, and you could tell he was trying to get away from something. This kept up for about 15 minutes. I guess this is what might be considered a night terror. The next morning, he didn't remember any of it. When I later told him my concern, he admitted that every night for years, he dreamed about the night he was ripped out of his parents' home and placed in the orphanage.

I did some research and saw that there wasn't much you could do for night terrors. The mind was trying to work things out, and as he matured, it would resolve itself. After thinking about it, I suggested that he should tell himself before he went to sleep that everything was okay and that the outcome was good. I thought maybe that would start helping to ease his mind. He said sometimes it worked.

I knew Carol and Stan's deaths hit him hard, but I told him that I was there for him. I had never been through anything like this before, but I knew our community would be there for one another and I knew I would be okay with time. He, on the other hand, wasn't okay. He told me he was, but in his head and heart, things were starting to unravel. Unfortunately, there were not many outward signs except that when he talked on the phone, he went outside in the yard. I questioned him on that, and I told him I was uncomfortable with it, but he blew me off. He was in his room a lot, but what teenager isn't? We were working together on the artwork for the cover of *From Half to Whole* and had just had a breakthrough in its design. I was happy; he seemed to like it, too. Those are his arms you see on the cover. That photo was taken the morning before his suicide attempt. He was mad at me the night of the incident because, as I stated in the beginning, after finding out he had a Facebook account without us knowing, I took his phone, his computer, and all other electronics away. There was tension between us because he said I "shut him out of his world."

As the day went on, things seemed normal around the house and with him until about 10:00 that night. I was working on the computer, and he came down to get tape. I asked him what he was doing, and he said he was working on an art project. A few minutes later I went to bed and heard a commotion outside my door. When I opened the door, I saw him taping some papers to it, but as quickly as I saw them, he was taking them down and running away. I thought it was weird, but drama was sometimes his middle name, and I was too tired to investigate. I thought I would deal with it in the morning. I slept really well, better than I had the whole month. I was having dreams, all of them different, but I woke up every morning with an uneasy feeling. The dreams made me feel as if something was going wrong but that it wasn't going to end terribly. Yet that night I didn't have any of them.

When I woke up to the 911 operator, I was shocked. Nothing like this had ever happened in any one of our families, so I truly didn't know what was about to unfold. I was panicked, angry, and mystified by the boy sitting on the bed with his head between his hands. He was lost and lonely. I knew that boy seven years ago, but not anymore. He had come such a long way. I felt that we had done so much right and he had so much to be proud of. It tore us all up.

The next few days in the hospital were tough. A lot of emotions were flowing through all of us, and we were angry. We couldn't understand, and we didn't know why he would do something so drastic.

When he came home, he wanted us to give him all kinds of freedom, but we were not thinking that way. We were tired of the games and the pain. I searched for ways to help him. Of course, so many people were calling. It was nice to hear the stories of how sweet he was and how many parents cried to me on the phone. I heard time and time again that he was the most respectful kid out of all of their children's friends. He helped with the groceries and always said "please" and "thank you." It was nice, this outpouring from the community. It was reminiscent of when the boys first came.

One phone call I knew I didn't want to make was to my girlfriend Maryanne. She adored Adrian, and he adored her. It was going to be tough to tell her the news. After the shock of it, she said that she wanted to help. I knew if anyone could get through to him, it would be her. When we picked him up at the hospital, he so was happy. He was rambling on about how he wanted to spend the weekend at my brother-in-laws house and what friends he wanted at the party we were going to have for him! I got the feeling he felt life was going to go right back to normal after we had a spectacular weekend.

Unfortunately, that wasn't going to be the case. When we first got home, we sat with him and went over the rules that were now set. This didn't sit well with him, and I could see him getting tenser and tenser as we spoke. I knew it was time for Maryanne to come over, and she did. She sat with him and went over each rule with him a little at a time and broke it down. She explained each of them and provided the reasoning behind our decisions and worked it out with him in which order he wanted things back. We had taken all things away and gave him timelines on when we would reevaluate the situation. She had him put the items in priority order of what he felt he wanted back the most and what he could wait on. I could see the tension lessen in him.

After she was done, we were invited to Gigi's house. This time we were not going to be chasing a dog through the neighborhood, that's for sure. She was having a dinner for a missionary priest who was in from Sierra Leone, Africa. His name is Fr. Themi, and his mission is to help the survivors of the twelve-year civil war that embarked on that country. The life of these people and what they have gone through was portrayed in the movie *Blood Diamonds,* featuring Leonardo DiCaprio. Because of the pain he helps heal every day, Gigi knew that he would be able to talk to Adrian and touch his soul.

So Maryanne, Adrian, and I went over and had a wonderful night. It was actually pretty magical. The energy in the room was light, and the laughter was abundant. It really broke the tension I had been dealing with all week. We tried different foods, and when the timing felt right, Adrian was asked to go in the other room and Fr. Themi spoke to him. It was a wonderful way to transition into our new way of life. He told me afterward that Adrian had a lot of trauma in his past and he was ready to start talking. And that's what he did.

Maryanne continued to talk to him for the majority of four days. She got him to open up as she guided him through his fears. One thing she did that was magical was she put him in the driver seat in her car and had him imagine that he was in his favorite car going anywhere he wanted, and when he wanted to leave that place, all he had to do was turn the wheel and go someplace else. Through visualization she had him go from place to place in his mind with his eyes closed. She would ask him questions, and he would tell her what was going on. As their "drive" unfolded, he began to sweat. She could see the fear and pain in Adrian's body language, and she would remind him he could "drive away" anytime he needed to. In that short half hour, after they were done, she could see him sweating. She was worried that he would hate her. But he actually said it felt good to open up. He was ready to talk because it felt good.

The next night, she and Adrian had a campfire in our backyard. One of his friends came over also. They wrote down their deep, dark secrets and threw them in the fire and watched them burn. That night, he said a world had been lifted off his shoulders. I believe my friend saved Adrian's life. To me she did more for him in those crucial few days than anything else he had encountered thus far. Once he opened up about the horrors that were going on in his mind, he realized talking about it wasn't so bad. He now sees a therapist to deal with post-traumatic stress stemming from his past.

Since this ordeal, Adrian has realized the love everyone has for him and that talking to someone is not so bad. I had always hoped for someone who would mentor my kids. I always saw the value in that, and Maryanne was finally in his life to fill this void. My hope for the future is to find such a program and implement it for adopted children. He is now, one and a half years later, much stronger because he has hit rock bottom and there is only one way up from there. We also have discussed with him that God has given him a third chance at life. It is now his job to be true to himself, his soul, and his family. And that whatever may be eating at him, it's easier to open up about it than to hold it in. The dreams that were haunting him are now less stressful for him. He said that now when he has them, he will get up, wash his face, and fall right back to sleep.

The following words are from Adrian. We hope that something within this letter helps you understand what a child in his situation might be thinking.

Adrian's Point of View

I'm not really sure what made me start thinking about suicide. I guess it was right around the time Stan and Carol died and I started to remember the feeling of losing people you really love and care about.

I used to not be able to sleep because I would get nightmares about my past.

I always wondered what the world would be like without me, and I never thought people would miss me at the time. I thought the end result would be that everyone would forget about me and move on, but after reading my text messages and seeing all the people that care about me, it made me change my mind about killing myself and after all the help I got from Maryanne D, I started to think about the positives in life.

I always wanted to see what the afterlife was about. I'm not sure what made it appealing to me. It was just always going through my head; all the thoughts of suicide started to not scare me, and after a couple of weeks, I started to think about it all the time. After everything was over, I started to think differently about life and all the things I would have left behind.

Right now I'm just trying to stay out of trouble and follow the rules. If I have a problem, I open up to my family, friends, and my counselor when before I only opened up to them about some things.

I HAVE ALWAYS TOLD MY KIDS THEY HAVE a right to be angry about what has happened to them. We would always be there to listen. This way I thought they would face their past and figure out a way to come to peace with it. Did it help? Sometimes when things are copasetic, I look at them and say to myself, "Wow, look what they have grown into and become. Look at how they have grown as athletes, and look at the artist Adrian has become," and so on. I wish their mom knew.

We have to admit it and let our kids know that giving them up is one of the hardest things in the world a woman can do. I know people assume that drugs and alcohol have a big part in them losing their children, and many adoptions do come from that type of environment. I wonder if the carelessness and dysfunction that goes on in the home up until the children are taken away is something those families even consider a threat. Nothing will ever replace that child, so why not fight harder and do what you need to do so that child and your family can stay together? The decision was made to have this child, wasn't it? I know it's easy for me to say, but it does baffle me. The fact is, not knowing where they are or what they've become IS something that will haunt you forever. And to me . . . it is not worth losing that fight.

On the other side, sometimes the harsh reality of their past hits these kids and there is no hiding from the pain they feel. I don't think we will ever understand those feelings. But in those moments, the boys need our strength more than ever. The day Adrian decided to end it all is when the pain and the noise in his head became all too much. He wanted the noise and the nightmares to go away.

This whole time, since the boys came, I have been very concerned about the day things might go sour. So I have always been looking for insight as to what I can do to help when the time came about. I have found a few things that I will go over below, but last summer, while on vacation, I found this book that really hit home with me. It was a book written by Vinny G. from *Jersey Shore*, called *Control the Crazy*. It made me understand that the chatter in someone's head can be overwhelming, and it's hard to shut it down. The book gave me a lot of insight into what was going on. Vinny writes about techniques that you can use to find the peace within yourself when the chatter becomes too much. He compares our mind's chatter to a computer screen that is overloaded with data and how you need to shut it down visually in your own mind. In fact, I have used this trick a few times since learning it. When the kids get to be too much, I take a deep breath and visualize a laptop with the screen open, and I visually slam it shut and it clears the thoughts. That and deep breathing are some of the ways to calm the mind because that split second of breathing and calming can be a split second of change for the better and may save a life. One last thing he talks about is remembering to be grateful. He says that when there is an angry thought, to think of a positive thought that you are grateful for because that one thought will knock out the negative. You can't have two thoughts in your head at once so the good will knock that bad one right out of the park!

Another program that I listened to last year was called "The Calm Parent". This set of CDs explains that each person has their "stuff," and with that we need to learn that their stuff belongs in their "box" so to speak. When you are dealing with your kids, it teaches you to remember that their issues belong in their box, unless of course it is a concern you need to focus on. Learning that has also been helpful to me. When we get into stupid arguments, I try to say "that belongs in his box, not mine." I then take a *deep breath, think a positive thought and try to move on.* I have to say it is working. I have also noticed I am much better at staying calm. When I am yelling, I can now stop myself and just speak, and I can tone it down easier than in the past.

Other stress relievers I have found are things like riding my bike, which is heaven on earth to me, and playing loud music when no one's around and dancing like a lunatic. That ends up making me laugh. I also have turned the music WAY UP in the car when the kids argue and won't stop. I zone into that, and it tunes them out. Of course, I am paying attention to the road at all times trying to survive the chaos that's going on around me, but I'm singing as loud as I can to drown them out. It must be a very funny sight from an outsider looking in.

Taking a shower is another relaxer for me; I can actually feel the stress wash out through my feet. After my shower, I lie down while still in the calmness of it all, with the warm feeling from the steam of the shower and take a quick nap. Naps to me are priceless. At times when everyone is at work and in school, I shut off the phone in my room and take a nap, sometimes a few minutes sometimes a few hours. My friends don't understand how I find time for it, but I do. It's important to me because it does a world of good for my soul. The point is, meditation, yoga, anything that gets you to concentrate on YOU is the most important gift you can give yourself and your family. When you start the day feeling refreshed and cared for, (or even in the middle part of the day when the kids get home), that does all of you good. It may only last a few minutes sometimes, but at least that few minutes weren't spent yelling.

Time spent with my friends is also high on the list of important things for me. Whether we go out to lunch or talk on the phone, they have turned my moods around numerous times, by either giving me a solution to my issue or reminding me that I am a good mom and wife. They remind me how well the kids are doing or will listen and sympathize when I don't know where the next moment in time is going to take me.

On the other hand, for the kids to stay sane, they need activity. Sports are a great outlet for them, and the coaches are a huge help in teaching them life lessons. I have said to coaches, "It's fine for you to bench them. Tell them what they are doing wrong because they don't listen to me!"

Sports get their energy out; it teaches them how to focus and teaches them to work as a team. On the other hand, something like tennis teaches them how to compete against themselves, and that also is a good lesson learned. I also think it helped them with the ADHD that we were told they have.

I remember in the beginning when Adrian played flag football, he would be in the huddle and looking at the butterflies! UGH! But now he is in the huddle working with the team and running the plays as the starting QB, kicker, punter, outside linebacker, and wide receiver. He's come such a long way!

David used to complain constantly that his team wasn't good enough; this kid did this, and this kid did that. We talked to him till we were blue in the face on how he wasn't the only person on the team and how everyone needs to learn. Now that, with maturity, has changed also. These are all signs of good coaching and good parenting.

A Therapist's Insight

The teenage years, as we all know, are a very confusing time for both the teenager and the parents. It is a complicated time—as the teen is trying to establish autonomy in decision making, he's also trying to "fit in" with his peer group. At the same time trying to figure out what he wants to look like, he also is confused on how he wants to act. The parent is trying to allow for some independence but still worries about the teen's ability to demonstrate good judgment and to make good choices. In the cases I have had, this stage of development seems be more complicated for the adopted child as the self-esteem seems to be even more fragile.

Unfortunately, suicide attempts, completed suicides, high-risk behaviors that sometimes end up fatal, are too common amongst teenagers. Warning signs that a child might be suffering with severe depression or anxiety might not be obvious. Try not to assume your child is okay because he "appears" to be okay. A child who is adopted is not necessarily at a greater risk for suicidal ideations, but is probably more at risk for depression and anxiety. Keep communication as open as possible with your child. While communication is a challenge unto itself, it is very difficult in the case where your child is defiant and has created a wall between his parents and himself. It is okay to ask your child if he ever feels sad and what are the things or situations that cause him to feel that way. Do not be afraid to ask your child if he has ever had suicidal thoughts or thoughts of harming himself. If so, do not panic. Seek out professional help for him.

Where have I been, and where am I going?

An essay from Adrian on his life, before and after his adoption.

I was born in Poland to a loving mom and dad. At this time I had one older brother and one older sister. My younger brother was born. Then when I was about three my mom and dad started to drink and do drugs. My older brother started a little after my parents did, and then after that I started, but stopped shortly after the policemen came to take me to an orphanage along with my two brothers and one sister. Within five years of being at the orphanage I started to get into more fights and became more violent to anyone who tried to get to know me. Before my parents from America adopted me with my younger brother, people tried to adopt me but I was too much for them to handle. I was always given back. When I came to America, I always got in trouble with the schools. I would tell my teachers off or I would be making fun of the kids in my class. Now I have changed somewhat. I am nicer and more caring. I love my mom and dad and I trust them; that's something I could never do with anyone after what happened to me when I was younger. I have made many friends in America. I asked a couple of my friends, family members, and kids from my sports teams what do they think of me? I was told funny, helpful, caring, fast, strong, stupid at times, daring, and very tall.

I am not a big fan of school but my favorite subject in school is gym, I like staying fit. Language arts and reading along with other subjects are great to learn but staying fit is like feeding a homeless guy pizza. They just love it and that's how I feel on being fit. After school ends in June, I love going to the shore, my family and friends do a lot down there. We play football on the beach or volleyball; it is a lot of fun. One of my mom's best friends lives there and she always has us over for dinner the first night we are down there. Her cooking is great and by the time we have to go home it feels like we were only down for a day. But we stay at one of our houses for two weeks, most times.

Along with going down the shore, I have many hobbies and sports I like to do. My hobbies are fishing, swimming, going to the gym, and walking the boardwalk with my friends when I am at the shore. I like going fishing with my uncle because it is fun. We get to talk about our lives and how our family was different without me. We always do bets on who can catch the biggest fish, but he always catches the smallest one so he says the bet was who can catch the smallest fish. I love doing things with my uncle. I like being with the earth and doing things with nature, but I also love sports, and I am told I am pretty good at them. The sports I play are soccer, football, wrestling, volleyball, and I am going to start baseball again.

Even though I love sports, I also love animals. I have two dogs and one big lizard. I love playing with them, and I miss them when I go on vacation every year. My dogs make me laugh when they sneeze or do some other funny things. My favorite place to go on vacation is the shore, I like going to Florida but *we go there way too much. One of the reasons I like the shore is because they have the best hot wings down there and they taste very good. My favorite restaurant is on the boardwalk and that's where I get my hot wings.*

After the summer I make goals that I try to accomplish within the year. My goals are not to get into any fights, stay fit for football, and do better in language arts. I am going to miss my eighth-grade year, but I am going to have so much fun at the shore this summer, going for runs in the morning and going for ice cream in the evenings. My favorite is going to the boardwalk from 9:00 in the morning to 12:00 at night. This year I am going to go to the gym more so I can be better in football so I can be great in high school, and maybe some good colleges will look at me for football. The biggest goal I want to achieve in high school is to be a great football player and after that be great in college. The job I want after college is being in the NFL.

Chapter 15

Adoptive families adopt, and adoptees adapt.

8 key rules for success.

There is so much advice out there about the best way to raise a family—how to keep everyone together as a unit and encourage your kids to grow—but I can only offer what I have found has worked best in our unique situation. I am reminded of a story I once read that has forever stuck in my mind.

It is about a hardworking man and his son.

> One evening, after a long day on the job, the man comes home. As he does every day, the boy asks him about his day. The man responds wearily, then is startled when his son prods him to find out how much his father's hourly wage is. Too tired to argue, the father tells the boy what he wants to know. A short while later the boy comes out of his room and asks his father for some money. Tired and thinking the boy is going to waste the money on something silly, the man scolds the boy. Soon after, the father regrets his fierce words and asks his son why he asked for the money. "To pay you for an hour of your time so we can spend some quality time together, Father," he said.

Your time is by far the single most important gift you can give to your children. Below are my eight ingredients for a happy and healthy "adopted" household.

1. Be around.

Right before we got the boys, Bernie had called to tell me he had a great job offer with a lot more money, but it would mean he needed to work in Long Island. Long Island is about three hours from our house, so it would mean he wouldn't be home every night. I thought about it, and I said, "You know, these boys are coming here for stability. If you leave three days a week or more, how are we giving them stability? What's the use? I couldn't handle them all without you, and this is not what we all signed up for." To this day, I know in my heart that not taking the offer was the best decision we ever made. I really believe that dinner around the table and a parent home when the kids get home is so vital to their growth. I know some families don't have that luxury, but we have fought to keep that true in our home.

These days, with companies allowing you to work from home, I think it's a good idea to either have one parent get that type of job or work it out so that someone is home a few days a week. I have found that "constant presence" is of the utmost importance. If both parents get home later than the child, then the child will go back to the unstructured life he knew so well. Add a cell phone to the mix, time alone in the house, Facebook, and Skype, and things can run rampant. It can feel like another type of abandonment to them, even though both of you are out working hard to give them what they need. I never wanted our kids to think, *I'm alone again. They left me just like my mom/dad left me. These people are no different. They just give me rules and punishments!* I feel that makes them disconnect and revert back to what they knew from their past. They'll think, *I don't need them. I survived this long without them,* and they will tap into their independent self, and you will have a tough time breaking down that wall. Be careful! There is nothing more powerful than a parent being home when they walk in the door.

Is it fun dealing with the school calling or the bus driver stopping you on the road to tell you your kid was bad? Did I love all the fighting

I had to deal with when they walked in the door, either between the two of them or about the homework they didn't want to do? No, it's not what I bargained for, but I wouldn't change it for anything in the world. Some of my memories now, later in life with my mother gone, are of walking in the door and smelling dinner on the stove and hearing her say, "Hi! How was your day?" I hope my children will think of this in the years to come when they run in and out of our lives while living their own lives. It warms me, and I hope it warms them.

Is it possible to be home when your child gets out of school or soon after? I don't know—only you know that—but it's something that, across the board, I hear people say they are happy they did once they've done it. Sometimes losing some income is made up for in other ways. You do become creative in how you handle your money, and in the end the rewards outweigh the negative.

2. Break bread together—every night, if possible.

Eating dinner together is also important to build a relationship with your adopted children; you learn a lot at the dinner table. It gives the children a sense of unity and family, and they are more likely to open their minds to more nutritious food and less likely to turn to drugs. I see in my family the unity of my nieces and nephews when we are together at meals during the holidays. In fact, last Thanksgiving my 20-year-old nephew said he couldn't imagine not growing up around the dinner table. My niece talked about how, when she was in college, she noticed so many kids had no real connection to their families. She felt sad for them because she couldn't imagine not being connected. I see how every one of them comes home for the holidays, and we are all so happy to see one another. That's the reason we want kids, isn't it? So they have a bond and they know there is a stable family behind them no matter what happens to them in life, right?

Now, I know this may be an issue for some people who work or don't cook, but when considering adoption, seriously think about reorganizing and see if you are open to restructuring your lives. Life as you know it now will be very different, but that isn't a bad thing. Without restructuring your work schedules and eating habits, it will be hard to have a structured and stable environment for these kids—or any kid, for that matter.

Has eating dinner at the table every night been a wonderful experience year after year? No! We have had many hard nights; nights I wanted to run away from the table because of all the mean things that were being said. All the disrespect I got when Bernie was not there for whatever reason shook me to my core.

3. Stay united with your partner.

In the book *Troubled Transplants*, author Richard J. Delaney talks about just that, the disrespect that an adopted or foster child may have toward the mother. One of the chapters shows a visual of a mother and her child. But it was not what you would expect. The image of the toddler was placed above the mother, and it was much larger than the image of the mother. He calls this a "reverse effect" and explains that this is when the child negatively influences the family. In the drawing, the mother is not holding the child; she is actually leaning her elbow on his leg with the look of defeat on her face. Seeing that image hit me like a ton of bricks! It was so powerful. To me it showed that adopted children felt so empowered over their mother, possibly because they had seen so much disrespect toward the mom in the past. Now being in a home where a mom and dad actually get along, this is not normal to them, so they try to change it, pitting the father against the mother because it is comfortable to them. It made me see what was happening in our own lives at the time.

I have seen adoptive parents who loved and respected each other prior to adoption falling into arguments and most of the time the mother feeling betrayed. This is something I will be talking about in my future program, advocating for the parents to agree on how to parent and to not place blame on one another. Mothers tend to bear the brunt of the disagreements, since they are with the children more often. The father needs to be aware of this so the family does not become divided. There is so much we go through to have these children, and to then become the underdog all the time is very disheartening, and it leaves the new family in a very fragile state.

4. Be open to outside resources.

At about this time, the *Total Transformation* program came miraculously into the picture, and it was the right time for me.

I was worn out from the uncivilized manners my kids showed during dinner. It was hard to sit there and watch Nathan having to deal with it, too. Nothing he said even helped to convince them they were out of line. It killed me because it made me question what happened to our family and how it was going to get better. The other day I asked Nathan if eating at the dinner table was something he enjoyed, and he said he now enjoys it, but for years it was hard to sit there because of all the chaos it caused. Even when we implemented chores in the kitchen after dinner, there were many tough nights. They took it as time to fight; the arguments and physical fighting that would ensue made it very difficult to think, relax, and enjoy an evening in our house. I'm happy to say that eventually, with a lot of effort and praying, that they changed and matured and grew into doing their jobs in a much more timely fashion with a lot less hassle attached! So when you are about to give up hope, "keep on truckin,'" as they used to say. You will get on the other side of this challenge at some point.

5. Get creative.

The next big issue we faced was getting our children to have a better taste palate when it came to the dinner table and what they chose to eat. I never make different meals for the kids; when something is put on the table, they need to try it and try to finish it. If they can't, then my husband will swap one thing that they like from his plate and eat what they don't like. Sometimes they moan and groan, but with most foods, not all, they end up eventually eating it. Are they happy that I make something they don't want? No, but just like with anything, you have to stick to your guns and choose which battles you want to fight. Will we all want to fight the same ones? I don't think so, but we have to always be weighing it out.

By giving them an array of foods to become familiar with, you have the opportunity to help fight obesity, and as time goes on, to have enjoyable dinners together. You get really good at hiding such things as lentils in the sauce—just puree it and no one knows the difference. You have just added more protein to your pasta meal. Do the same with eggplant and other things. Just make sure there's no evidence left behind or seen in the sauce. Also add some pureed beans to the stuffed pepper mixture. A new thing we have added into the mix is when David doesn't like something, he gets to have a salad instead. He loves salad, and I'm okay with that since he is getting something that's good for him. What's funny is that I've realized once we give them a choice, they only use it once or twice and then they don't seem to ask about it anymore.

That reminds me of a time when Adrian used to be a crazy man running around the house being obnoxious. One day I finally figured out that if I let him go in to the Jacuzzi room to scream and act funny all by himself for a few minutes with no one around, it would fulfill his need. I told him that I felt relieved I wouldn't have to watch his craziness anymore, and he could get it all out. My only rule was that he wasn't allowed to scream in a way that would make someone think he was getting murdered. Guess what? He did it once, and he never did it again. It's funny to me how it takes us so long to come up with these ideas, and once it's implemented—in my house, anyway—it falls to the wayside in one shot! UGH! Why can't I just think of these things a little sooner and with a lot less stress?

6. Let them explore their past.

A question that I don't know will ever be answered is: Do the kids feel connected to us or is there always an "invisible being" disconnecting us? That "invisible being" being their birth mom, dad, or both. Will we ever know for sure we are truly connected? I can say this: I have been to many conferences where adopted children get up and speak, and they all have great respect for the adoptive parents. The feeling that comes across is that they are being raised by people who truly love them, and they recognize that. I know in my own family we have an older relative that was adopted, and he feels nothing but respect for his parents and does not care to look into his past to find out the truth of the matter.

Do all adopted children want to know their past? I'm not sure I could say yes to that; with that said, I also feel that you should *not* feel threatened by it if they do want to search. You are giving them a life they otherwise would not have, and without that, even though they hate us at times, they know they would not have the life they have now without us.

7. Keep the lines of communication open— but don't push.

I always felt it was important that they know they can talk to us. When conversations about the past come up, usually in the car, they seem to feel that they can speak freely. That openness helps everyone feel more comfortable and the conversations have gotten easier as time goes on. They are comfortable to talk about it, and that's so important.

As you can imagine, we were shocked when Adrian tried to commit suicide. I crumbled not knowing where we went wrong. Why did he shut down? I had talked to him about our friends' deaths. I let him know it was going to be tough, but together we would get through it. I guess he didn't hear my words, and for that I am truly sorry. Now when we go to therapy together we discuss our points of view, or should I say, argue our points of view, but we walk out of there without any hate for each other. He is a bit more argumentative these days, being 16 and all, so he is testing our patience like all kids. We have also noticed that when one child calms down, another starts to act up. I just think to myself, *My parents went through it with six! I surely hope I survive three!*

Obviously, they don't like to talk to us about everything. Homework and things like that are tough, but we have figured out which of us is better at communicating on tough issues with each child, and that helps to minimize the fighting. Is the line of communication always wonderful? No, it isn't. As they grow more into teenagers, we have our battles as all families do, and I struggle with the looks and the attitudes, but I think when it comes down to the nitty-gritty, we all pull together, and they know we are here.

Do my kids sometimes think I'm mean and wish I didn't give them rules? HELL, YES! We may fight and argue, but I feel better when I call the hotline for *Total Transformation* if I need to talk to someone. I also put my iPod on and listen to the chapter on what I feel will solve my problems. The answers always seem to be there, and that helps me to take a step back and feel better about how I'm going to handle things next time. As I've said before, I try the different techniques to calm down as quickly as I can and make sure I get my point across.

One thing I know and try to take away from their clues is that as time goes on, they don't want to talk about or be reminded of the past anymore. It is something we need to be aware of as we listen to them. Sometimes I worry that their past can still influence them and I panic, probably unnecessarily, but it is something that concerns me. Rightfully so, because there is an added layer of challenges added to their lives.

I have heard adoptive families *adopt,* and adoptees *adapt.* I've noticed this to be true. The kids act very much like normal kids, with their moods, their attitudes, and so on. So how are we supposed to know what's going on if they don't talk when we ask? I hope in my heart that when they get angry about their situation as they get older, we feel we handled things the right way because there is no handbook guiding us through. There is nothing printed out on step-by-step parenting, let alone parenting an adopted child. I do feel though that when they talk about their past, their pain, and whatever else they are struggling with, we are comfortable to face the issues with them. We will be able to lift them up where it is needed and comfort them when they are down. That's why some type of support system is so important as you go through all of this. You cannot do it all alone. You need guidance through the turbulence, and I can attest to that! The other nice thing is when you're out of the stage of pulling your hair out, there's someone there to tell you that you look more together and not so frazzled. That's when you know, for maybe a moment, that you made it through.

8. Coach them on how to handle the "adoption" subject with peers.

A frustration for me when the boys were in school was hearing that my kids were getting ridiculed about being adopted. My suggestion to them was to come up, through role-playing, with something they were comfortable saying that stopped the person in his tracks. One thing I have heard David say is, "It could be any of you who ended up adopted. It just happened to be me." It's a great idea. It empowers them, and hopefully they carry that with them into the future if it ever comes up again.

When I watch a show like *The Locator,* it really hits home with me as to what these women go through, and the pain stays with them forever. We cannot push that aside when talking to our children. It is a reality, and I feel they need us to validate their birthmothers' pain. It may help their healing process, it shows them that "invisible being" that may be disconnecting us is accepted in our home. Yet on the other hand, I wonder if by putting the birthparents on a so called "pedestal," it makes the children feel that they were seen as bad children and that's why the family broke apart. Also, I wonder if sometimes that makes us, the adoptive parents, the bad guys because we discipline and have to set boundaries knowing they hate us for it. We see this as love and the chance for them to grow up with the knowledge of right and wrong, but do they see it that way? Are we the bad guys because we have rules? I know I have said to them that there are either rules or no rules in a household, really, there is no in between. But I am starting to feel that WE ARE THE HEROS in their lives as it was pointed out to me recently. We are always here; we pick up the pieces and guide them day after day so why do we put others on a pedestal?

We see them through thick and thin. We don't leave.

After the suicide attempt, I felt very angry at what happened to them in their past life, and I was also angry that while we are here trying to pick up the pieces, their other family has no knowledge of what they have truly done to these kids. I'm at odds with how I feel about how I would handle the conversation if I ever get the chance to talk to them.

A Therapist's Insight

Most of the clients I have had who were adopted did not have a need to search for their birthparents because they were living their lives with happiness and contentment. They feel all their needs are met and their adoptive parents are their parents. In fact, in most cases, the reason for seeking out counseling was not because they had issues surrounding their adoption. However, with deeper analysis, it became evident, in some cases, that the current issues they were struggling with were connected to their adoption but most clients learn how to work through this struggle.

Chapter 16

Caring for Special Needs Adoptees

Medication Dilemmas and Insights, Adopted and Biological
Children, The Similarities and the Differences

By Barbara Jean Keane, M.S.W., L.C.S.W.

SPECIAL NEEDS

Usually, prospective adoptive parents are asked if they would be interested in adopting a child with "special needs." Even though you might be told that the child that has been "assigned" to you is healthy, both psychologically and physically, developmental disabilities and/or learning disabilities could emerge later on. It is very important to intervene and seek out help early on if you begin to have concerns about your child's development or behavior.

MEDICATION DILEMMA

While medications can be useful in treating certain conditions, they can also be harmful and can increase the very problems they are intended to treat. I have had the opportunity to work with many children, adolescents and adults in my practice, some of whom are adoptive parents or are adoptees. Some were taking medication for anxiety, depression, or attentional difficulties. I admire Regina and Bernie for several reasons. The fact that they fight their "battles" with Adrian and David "naturally," without considering medicating them, should be noted. Their consistency and persistence in managing each difficult situation they have faced with Adrian and David, together, has helped them endure. However, every child and every situation is different, and sometimes, medication, in the short term, can be beneficial to the child.

In my own case as an adoptive parent and not as a therapist, our family was faced with the fact that we were told that our angel, who was one and a half months old when he was "assigned" to us, was born healthy at seven pounds. However, he struggled with anxiety, depression, learning difficulties, school phobia, and absence seizures. Because of all of these issues, we decided to consult with a psychiatrist. Abilify (Aripirazole) was one medication that was prescribed to our son. Unfortunately, he now suffers with an additional condition called Tardive Dyskinesia (TD), a movement disorder that is usually caused by medications like Abilify, or other antipsychotics.

Many people never experience any serious side effects from medications. But the longer the person is taking this type of medication (an antipsychotic) the greater the risk of developing this chronic and permanent condition. I wish I knew then what I know now. I use what I have learned through my own experience to help my clients navigate through their own journeys. I am so much more aware of the hidden risks behind medication also that, at any time, a side effect can surface that can change a child's life permanently. Medications, however, are sometimes necessary and can be beneficial in improving an individual's quality of life.

Regardless of these challenges my husband and I continue to have in raising our son, we love him, and will always love him. We could not imagine any other child to be ours. I continue to be excited to be his mother as I have been told by other parents who have had struggles in their lives.

INSIGHTS, ADOPTED AND BIOLOGICAL CHILDREN: THE SIMILARITIES AND THE DIFFERENCES

The process of adoption, like pregnancy, is exciting. It can take years from the time you have made the decision to adopt, to the end, when you are finally embracing your child. The process is always much longer than the average nine-month pregnancy. Most adoptive parents I have worked with say that during the waiting time, the anticipation of getting the child is a lot. They experience both excitement and fear that something might "go wrong." Most often, the prospective adoptive parent and the pregnant parent question their own ability to handle all the responsibilities of raising a child.

It became evident to me when I was in session with one of my clients many years ago that some people have difficulty understanding how the love for an adopted child can be the same as the love for a biological child. I remember sharing with this client how strong my love was for our son who was adopted. She responded, "If you feel that way toward your son, can you imagine how you would feel if he was really yours!" At first, this comment took my breath away! Then I remember feeling sad. I soon realized that we cannot expect someone to understand how the love can be the same. How can they truly know this, unless they, too, have experienced an adoption journey? That is, to finally hold the child in their arms who they have been anxiously waiting a very long time for. It is unfortunate that there are some people, for a variety of reasons, who have difficulty understanding love, let alone the love adoptive parents feel towards the child they've waited so long for.

Acknowledgments

There are so many people to thank—people who have supported me through thick and thin. So many conversations with friends and family pulled me through the roughest of times and got me to see that our story needed to be told. I'm so grateful to all of you, and you know who you are. You are all truly appreciated in my life.

I know that without the support of our Mastermind group, this book would have never made it! Thank you all for your great support, encouragement, and hours spent listening to me.

Of course, without Huminska's Anioly and her team here and in Poland, the adoption process would have never happened—and thus no story to tell. So thank you for all you did for us during that time, Mimi.

Once I started writing, Mary Choteborsky became a big part of the process. She walked me through various stages and gave me guidance until the end. Her knowledge of the industry and the editing aspect helped make the process seamless.

Thank you also to the following people, who have helped so much on a different level. They can't be forgotten.

Sandi DeFalco, Dauna Mays, Alyssa Radomski and Barbara Booth for your vast knowledge of editing. You supported my every step and never lost patience! To Sandi, for your help with the cover. And to you, Barbara—your encouragement from the beginning to start this book and for all your insight at the end has truly helped me pull this all together. Thank you!

Elizabeth Tunnicliffe for layout and production, I can't thank you enough for fitting my project into your busy schedule and making it a work of art. You are so talented.

Gigi Souritzidis, thank you for helping me in a pinch. You saved me countless hours!

Beata Roefaro, for the countless hours you spent with me on the phone discussing issues all these years and giving me the right information on the Polish side of things.

Barbara Jean Keane, thank you for adding "just enough" insight and for wanting to be a part of this book.

Jim Kukral, at JFK Services, you have been an asset to me for your marketing knowledge. I can't wait to see where this all ends up. You had so much patience this past year. It was tough, but you didn't get annoyed with my situation, and for that I thank you.

Eclipse, E.F. Studios, you were so fun to work with! You made me feel like a star! The audiobook, when it comes out, will kick ass, and it will be better than what we've listened to ourselves. I have confidence in us. Thank you so much.

And last but not least, thank you to my family, my husband, and my kids for supporting me in this endeavor from the cover to the final copy. Putting this out there was brave of all of you.

RESOURCES I RECOMMEND

FOR INFORMATIVE SUPPORT IN NJ: New Jersey Adoption Resource Clearing House (NJARCH) www.njarch.org

Concerned Persons for Adoption (CPFA) www.cpfanj.org

FOR POLISH ADOPTIONS: Mimi Huminski
Email: mhangels@adoptionspolish.com
www.adoptionspolish.com

TOTAL TRANSFORMATION AND VITAMIND: Visit my site, under PRODUCTS I RECOMMEND, at http://www.reginaradomski.com

Made in the USA
Charleston, SC
19 August 2014